I0828329

FIRE ON THE MOUNTAIN

FIRE ON THE MOUNTAIN

THE UNDEFEATED 1985 SAND ROCK WILDCATS

DOUGLAS SCOTT WRIGHT

Published by The History Press
Charleston, SC 29403
www.historypress.net

First published 2010

ISBN 9781540234575

Library of Congress Cataloging-in-Publication Data

Wright, Douglas Scott.
Fire on the mountain : the undefeated 1985 Sand Rock Wildcats / Douglas Scott Wright.
p. cm.

1. Football--Alabama--Sand Rock--History. 2. Sand Rock Wildcats (Football team) 3. Sand Rock High School (Sand Rock, Ala.)--Football. 4. School sports--Alabama--Sand Rock--History. I. Title.
GV959.53.S36W75 2010
796.3320761'65--dc22
2010001396

Notice: The information in this book is true and complete to the best of our knowledge. It is offered without guarantee on the part of the author or The History Press. The author and The History Press disclaim all liability in connection with the use of this book.

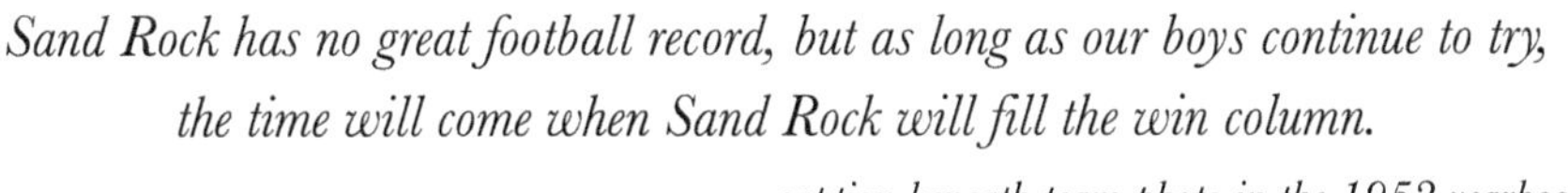

Sand Rock has no great football record, but as long as our boys continue to try, the time will come when Sand Rock will fill the win column.

—caption beneath team photo in the 1952 yearbook

CONTENTS

FOREWORD

Russell "Rusty" Jacoway, a husband, father and grandfather, is a great football coach and a mentor to many young men. In a short period of his life he has become one of the finest coaches in the state of Alabama.

I first met Coach Jacoway in 1983 at a local coaches meeting. At that time he was a cocky guy and looked like he was still in high school. But after listening to him, I discovered he was a very mature and knowledgeable person. I thought to myself, "He is either going to be very successful, or bomb out, as a football coach." At the end of his first season, he was 0-10, but his team continued to show improvement in every game. The next year, the program really started to turn around and made it to the second round of the state playoffs. Then, the 1985 team won the first-ever state championship in Cherokee County.

Coach Jacoway holds the best record of all coaches in the history of Sand Rock High School. I am proud to say that he is a fine, upstanding Christian man and coach, respected and admired by his players and peers. I predict that in the future he will be inducted into the Alabama High School Athletic Association's Hall of Fame. It will be a well-deserved honor, and it will also serve to honor the memory that so many people around here still have of the incredible football team he put on the field twenty-five years ago.

Coach Bobby Joe Johnson
Centre, Alabama
January 2010

PREFACE

If anyone who ever alleged to be a writer possessed the familiarity, not to mention the motive, to compose a hatchet job about either the Sand Rock Wildcats or Russell Jacoway, surely it would be me. My Cedar Bluff teammates and I lost to them twice in 1985 by a combined score of 28–13. When we played to a scoreless tie at the end of regulation in the regular season, we knew that we had a pretty good team. When we played again, ten games later in the second round of the state playoffs, we were still a pretty good football team. The Wildcats, on the other hand, had become something entirely different. Probably the angriest I had ever been at anybody in my life, up to that point, was at Russell Jacoway on Friday, November 15, 1985. Years later, I was fortunate enough to have the chance to meet Coach Jacoway, and his attitude and friendliness quickly helped me get past my adolescent rage. I am grateful for that first experience with him and for all the others that followed. Obviously, I could not have completed this book without his cooperation and infinite patience.

When my editors at The History Press first mentioned the idea of writing a book about high school football in Alabama, I immediately thought of the Wildcats. Just from memory, I knew that their story was impressive: an undefeated season and state title with a young head coach only two years removed from a ten-game losing streak. After dozens of interviews with Coach Jacoway, Assistant Coaches James Rowe and

Roland Hendon and more than a dozen players, I was sure that I had compiled the essential elements of a story that would appeal to just about anyone, regardless of whether or not they considered themselves football fans. All I had to do was tell it properly. I hope readers will judge that I have.

From my many hours of interviews I learned that, to a man—and the boys from that championship season are in their early forties now—the Wildcats appreciated and respected their head coach. I kept expecting a former player to throw him under the bus for some past indiscretion or release twenty-five years of pent-up frustration in a flood of profanity and then beg me to erase my recorder. If anyone had said a bad word about Jacoway, Rowe or Hendon, I would have printed it simply in the interest of fairness and accuracy. No one did. It seems hard to believe that a football coach as dedicated, hardworking and successful as Russell Jacoway didn't offend *someone* along the way. I suspect that he did. Perhaps any ruffled sensibilities have been smoothed over by the passage of time and those wonderful, unforgettable memories of winning the whole damned thing.

The written record of Sand Rock's run to the state championship is sparse. Most local newspapers either did not or could not adequately cover Cherokee County, Alabama, in 1985, and regional papers had larger audiences to consider when it came time to assign beat reporters on Friday nights. As a result, many of the recollections in this book came from one-on-one interviews with the men and women who experienced a portion of the Wildcats' history firsthand. From over thirty hours of interviews, I was able to compile a collection of many more memories than my allotment of pages allowed me to share, so I have attempted to choose the most relevant, interesting, hilarious and emotionally moving from among them. Hopefully, I was able to include something that will appeal to everyone. Wherever I attempted to re-create an active narrative, I depicted thoughts and attitudes as accurately as possible based on my interviews, with a minimum of creative supposition. Any errors of fact, tone or intent are mine.

My employers, David and Elizabeth Crawford, granted me much latitude to complete my extracurricular writing assignments, and I am grateful. My dedicated coworker, Tina Arnold, covered for me during

1985 Sand Rock Wildcats

Alabama Class 1A Champions

Seniors

Dwain Boyd
Dewayne Heard
Artie Mackey
Lance Mackey
Mark Parker
Jamie Pitts
Clayton Robertson
Chris St. Clair
Jim Tom Stimpson
Lyndon Tidwell
Jeff Whaley

Juniors

Dan Andrews
Phil Bryant
Scott Norris
David Rollins
Rickey Snider
Tommy Steele
Craig Twilley

Sophomores

Steve Allen
Mark Clanton
Toby Clanton
Woodie Clanton
Lamar Gifford
Shawn Giles
Eric Mackey
Sam McCoy
Jay Morgan
Joe Oliver
Jeff Prater

Freshmen

Joey Beard
Andy Gifford
Lou Honaker
Todd Morgan
Greg Parker
Kevin Reese
Eric Roebuck
Tommy Rowe
Bert St. Clair
Mark Wallace
Larry Wright

Managers

Michael Richardson
Stacy Manley
Johnny Moses
Lance Bryant

Coaches

Russell Jacoway
James Rowe
Roland Hendon

The 1985 Sand Rock Wildcats.

all those Monday afternoons when I was at home in front of this laptop instead of sitting at the desk next to hers. Thanks, also, to Sarah Benefield, Jerry Benefield and Kerry Mackey for reading early drafts and correcting my mistakes. The employees in the research department at the Gadsden Public Library endured more than their share of inane requests, and I appreciate them for never calling security. Dozens of other individuals assisted me along the way, some during lengthy sit-downs and others in brief conversations conducted in hallways or from adjoining tables in restaurants. Every tiny piece of information that they shared helped make this book better. For anyone who loves music from the '80s, it is my hope that a few of the chapter titles will set some toes to tapping.

I hope that the men who were still only "boys, good boys" when they won the Class 1A state championship twenty-five years ago will not regret entrusting me with a few of their most precious memories. I believe that I had as much fun telling their story as they did living it.

Chapter 1

THE END

By the time they filed off their chartered bus and onto the chilly campus at Repton High School sometime in the early afternoon on December 6, 1985, the forty-odd members of the Sand Rock Wildcat football team had exceeded just about everyone's wildest dreams—those of their fans in Cherokee County, their fellow students in the hallways back at school and possibly even the few among their families and friends who had not made the three-hundred-mile trip to south Alabama. But they had yet to meet their own expectations. To this day, many of those players and coaches insist that they had felt fairly positive for many months that they would earn their chance to play for the Class 1A state championship. Senior flanker Jeff Whaley's recollection is typical. "I remember talking about it just before we stepped onto the field for the first practice that summer," he said. "Valley Head had won it the year before, and we felt like the 1985 season was going to be our turn."

Before deciding if such confidence sounds boastful, first consider the facts. The previous few seasons had been a tough slog for Whaley and the other seniors who endured them. As ninth graders in the fall of 1982, Lance Mackey, Jamie Pitts, Dewayne Heard, Jim Tom Stimpson and Chris St. Clair were among the handful of players who had gone 1-9 for Jim Lowery in his final season as coach of the Wildcats. A year later, Whaley, along with Dwain "Bubba" Boyd, Artie Mackey and Clayton Robertson, joined their sophomore classmates on the field. But new coach Russell

Jacoway's first season at Sand Rock had been even worse than Lowery's last. Ten times the tousle-haired young man marched his players onto the football field, and ten times the team shuffled off a loser. The Wildcats sniffed victory in the first game before falling to cross-county rival Spring Garden, 8–6, and it was all downhill from there. The previous season, the opening game against the Panthers had produced Lowery's only win of the year, and Assistant Coach Roland Hendon feared what losing to the same team meant for Jacoway's chances for success in 1983. "I was afraid it was going to be a bad season," he said.

Hendon was right. The offense was abysmal, managing only fifty points all year, and the defense gave up over twenty points per game. With the exception of a narrow 15–12 loss in week ten, a glance at the season statistics makes it appear as though the Wildcats never even got close. Hendon knew that feeling a little too well—as a quarterback at Meek High School in the 1960s, he had lost the exact same number of games over the course of his junior and senior seasons. "After going 0-19 as a player and then losing nineteen in a row as an assistant coach, I was about ready to give up," he said.

But neither Hendon nor any of the mostly winless Wildcats called it quits after that horrific '83 campaign. In fact, lousy numbers and lopsided losses are not what stick out most in Hendon's mind today when he recalls Russell Jacoway's first football team. "You just had the feeling, all through the year, that we were getting better," Hendon said. "The kids always felt like they had a chance to win, and they played hard." A year later, boosted in part by an off-season weightlifting and conditioning program more productive and practical than anything they had ever experienced before, those kids played even harder.

The turnaround began in the fall of 1984. Also, the junior class was supplemented by the additions of Mark Parker and Lyndon Tidwell, whose more experienced teammates had become sick and tired of losing and let it show on the field. After eight games, the Wildcats were well on their way to completing a total about-face: six wins and only two losses, a total offensive output of 191 points and a defense that was allowing only 15 points per game. Whatever Jacoway, Hendon and defensive coordinator James Rowe were teaching was beginning to take hold, with the exception of one collapse early in the season—a 48–7 loss to Valley

The 1985 Sand Rock Wildcats, coached by Russell Jacoway, James Rowe and Roland Hendon, were the first Class 1A team in Alabama to go 15-0. *From the scrapbook of Jim Tom Stimpson.*

Head. Following an open date in week nine, the Wildcats won their season finale and then whipped Madison Academy in the opening round of the playoffs to earn another crack at the team that had embarrassed them in week three.

The game did not turn out as planned, though; Sand Rock lost a heartbreaker in the final minute, 17–16. Still, Jacoway's somewhat unconventional system was soundly in place, and the team had bought into his coaching philosophy. After Valley Head went on to capture the Class 1A state title in December 1984, the Wildcats began to realize that they had all the skills they needed to win every game of the coming season. Jacoway knew it, too. The front page of the Wildcats' playbook featured a short letter from the head coach addressed to the "Sand Rock Wildcats, 1985 Alabama State Football Champions."

Several months and fourteen straight victories later, the bus ride to Repton began about 8:00 a.m., following an early morning pep rally in the postage stamp–sized gymnasium at Sand Rock School. There was nowhere for the players to sit in the packed bleachers, so they plopped down in metal folding chairs along the baseline while the cheerleaders cheered and visiting parents and grandparents applauded. After the shouting died down, the entire community lined Alabama Highway 68 to wave pompoms and show their support with homemade signs and car horns. If video evidence from the game that night is any indication, most of those people hopped into their cars and headed south after the team bus motored past. The Wildcats might have been a long way from home by kickoff time, but they did not run up and down that distant gridiron alone.

The eight-hour journey was quiet, for the most part. Jacoway had been very clear that the drive to Repton was a business trip, not a joy ride. As the bus pulled out, he urged his players to keep their mind on the task at hand. "Concentrate on what we've learned and think about the job you have to do tonight," he told them. In the back, players drowned out the whine of the asphalt with headsets belting out the latest releases from Dire Straits and John Cougar Mellencamp on cassette tape or by going over play calls and blocking assignments with their seatmates. A few of the younger players got a little rowdy once or twice along the way, but Jacoway or one of the eleven seniors quickly quieted the racket. Tomorrow morning, everyone could goof off all he wanted, but tonight there was a job to do and it was time to focus. At one point near the end of the trip, tailback Jim Tom Stimpson looked up from his playbook, saw moss hanging from the tree limbs whizzing past his window and realized just how far from home he and his teammates really were. "It was like a different planet," he said.

A lack of sufficient funds necessitated the same-day trip. Earlier in the week, Jacoway had told the players that the athletic department's money situation was tight. He then allowed them to choose between motel rooms the night before the game or personalized satin jackets for Christmas. "They wanted the jackets, so we spent pretty much all day on a bus," Jacoway said. "That was okay, because other coaches had already told me the team would never have gotten a good night's sleep away from home." Following a pre-game meal at a roadside motel and an impromptu team meeting beneath a nearby outdoor pavilion, the motor coach pulled through the gate at Repton High School and between two narrow fences near the football field. Repton players leaning along both boundaries "were acting pretty wild," Jeff Whaley remembered. Whaley laughed out loud moments later when he saw Dwain "Bubba" Boyd's response to Repton's attempt at intimidation. The hard-hitting linebacker ripped off his jersey, held it up to the window for the skulking Bulldogs to see and screamed "Come to me!"

Lance Mackey had his own confidence in the Wildcats' impending strong performance reinforced outside the locker room a few minutes later. As Mackey and his teammates shuffled into their assigned dressing area, he spotted something he felt compelled to share with his head coach. "I just saw three of their players smoking in the parking lot," Mackey told Jacoway. "We've got this game won already!" Jacoway may have been only a few years older than his starting quarterback, but he knew it was going to take more than a handful of winded players to ensure a victory over a team that had trounced number one–ranked Beulah in the semifinals the week before.

During the pre-game broadcast, one Mobile, Alabama television announcer described the Repton Bulldogs as "a good bit bigger and, I believe, more rugged" than the Wildcats. Sure enough, Jacoway's starting offensive guards only weighed about 135 pounds apiece. As Jacoway had explained to local media outlets several times in the days leading up to the game, Chris St. Clair and Jamie Pitts were about to square off against a defensive lineman almost as big as both of them put together. At six feet, eight inches tall and 260 pounds, Repton's Tommy Dukes was a giant by high school football standards of the time and had already signed a scholarship to play college basketball. Jacoway told *Gadsden Times* sportswriter Greg Bailey that he had confidence in his guards because "they get off the ball and get in your face." Still, he conceded that it would not be easy for St. Clair and Pitts to manhandle someone as big and strong as Dukes, whose face they could barely have reached while standing on a stepladder. "It will be a challenge for them," Jacoway told the *Times*.

WYNI Radio sports director Stewart Young handled the play-by-play for the Class 1A championship game. Young, sporting a full beard and the feathered hairstyle that defined the 1980s, was on assignment for a Monroeville, Alabama cable TV company that had contracted to broadcast live audio and video of the game to its subscribers. Young shared the booth that night with David Johnson and Terry Teat. Johnson, a slight man in his mid-fifties sporting a maroon coat and tie, was principal at Repton High School. The much younger Teat, who had been invited over from the Sand Rock sideline to provide in-game color commentary, was dressed much more casually. Teat may not have been wearing his Sunday best, but the public address announcer for Sand Rock's home games knew the Wildcats better than anybody else for at least two hundred miles. If Lance Mackey started peppering the air with passes, Teat would know the names of the players who were hauling them in.

During the pre-game show, Young asked Johnson and Teat to discuss each team's strengths. Teat immediately mentioned Sand Rock's stout defense and potent passing game; Johnson said he felt the Bulldogs could play defense as well as the Wildcats but admitted that he was scared of the Wildcat quarterback and receivers. "I'm quite sure they are going to throw the ball, and they do it well," he said. His breath clearly visible as he spoke—and ignoring a thousand fans crammed into the bleachers, every one of them huddled under blankets and wearing gloves and heavy coats—Johnson insisted that the temperature, hovering in the low forties, would not be a factor: "It's not bad weather, just good football weather." Repton High School closed in 1989, but if its doors were open today superstitious Bulldogs fans might still be arguing whether Johnson's next words conjured up the curse that doomed their team to lose: "It's going to be a defensive struggle, so the team with fewer turnovers is probably going to win the game."

Proof positive that the Wildcats were not on their own so far from home came when the Sand Rock faithful swarmed the field and formed a one-hundred-yard-long victory line along the visitor's sideline just before kickoff. The home-standing Bulldogs, decked out in maroon jerseys, gray pants and undecorated white helmets, only managed a forty-yard gauntlet of fans. Just before their teammates jogged from one end zone to the other, Sand Rock captains Jim Tom Stimpson and Jeff Whaley walked side by side to midfield for the coin toss. They wore white uniforms with maroon trim, and each had his arm around a maroon helmet emblazoned with a brush script "Wildcats." Towering over them at the fifty-yard line was Dukes, one of the Repton captains. Whaley remembered looking up at the massive lineman and wondering what he and his teammates had gotten themselves into. A little over two hours later, as he limped back to the Bulldogs' locker room after a night spent swatting undersized offensive linemen away from his knees and ankles, Dukes must have been having similar thoughts.

After taking the opening kickoff, Sand Rock's offense stalled about midfield, then Repton fumbled the ball right back to the Wildcats on their first play from scrimmage. The Bulldogs did the same thing on the next possession—two offensive plays, two fumbles. In the press box, Principal Johnson suddenly had second thoughts about his pre-game weather analysis. "Maybe it's cold hands," he said. But Sand Rock couldn't capitalize on either turnover. Each team ended up with four first-quarter tries at the end zone and a zero on the scoreboard. Johnson, ever the optimist, declared that his team had been down this road before. He said that the 12-2 Bulldogs "have been out-manned and maybe played a few teams better than they are, but they always find a way to win."

From the opening snap, Sand Rock's offensive line had little success controlling Tommy Dukes. Several times in the first half, starting tailback Jim Tom Stimpson took the handoff, accelerated to the line of scrimmage and then disappeared beneath a moving billboard wearing jersey no. 75. "Every time we came up to the line of scrimmage Dukes would switch sides," Lance Mackey said. "He'd walk back and forth so we couldn't figure out how to block him." Mackey often delayed his cadence as long as possible, hoping to get a read on where Dukes was going to line up. Whenever he got the chance, Mackey called out a signal that switched the play to the opposite side of the field from Dukes. "I remember going to the line of scrimmage once," Mackey said, "and Chris St. Clair, one of our guards, was looking back at me shaking his head as if to say 'there's no need to run the play we just called, let's try something else.'"

For Sand Rock, "something else" usually meant throwing the ball. Today, given the popularity of the spread option that permeates all levels of organized football, the Wildcats' offense from the mid-1980s seems quaint by comparison. But twenty-five years earlier, Russell Jacoway's power-I alignment, supplemented by a quarterback who could roll out and accurately fire off twelve to fifteen passes a game, often confounded coaches who did not have the time or talent to teach more than the most simplistic forms of pass defense. Instead, coaches in those days relied on 5-3 or 6-2 defensive alignments designed specifically for stopping the run and hoped that they never faced a talented passer. Usually, even if a team was lucky enough to have a player who could throw the ball, there was no one else on the team who could catch. Not usually, anyway.

Early in the second quarter, with Dukes dominating the line of scrimmage, Jacoway decided that it was time for a change of pace. On third and ten from his own forty-four, Mackey fired a completion down the middle of the field to his cousin, Artie Mackey, at the Bulldogs' thirty-three. "That seems to be working," Teat analyzed succinctly from the press box. The passing game paid off again three plays later, when Mackey found Dewayne Heard just inside the twenty. Another pass to Heard on second down moved the ball inside the ten-yard line. From there, Boyd pounded the ball down to the seven for Sand Rock's sixth first down of the game. Three plays later, Stimpson scooted in from a yard out. The point-after kick by junior Tommy Steele gave the Wildcats all the points they would need to win.

Repton almost tied the game on the next possession. After the Sand Rock defense stopped an off-tackle run on third down, the Bulldogs lined up to punt but instead ran a fake and kept the drive alive with their only pass completion of the game. Temporarily rejuvenated on a night that would end up spoiled by their own mistakes, the Bulldogs converted another fourth down near the Sand Rock twenty-yard line and finally drove into the end zone with 2:15 left in the half. For some reason, veteran coach Hugh Wilson chose to try a two-point conversation, but "Bubba" Boyd stuffed a dive play to the fullback just short of the goal line. The offenses swapped possessions in the final minutes before Sand Rock picked off a pass to end the half.

Throughout the third quarter, Sand Rock's defense bent but did not break. Several Bulldog drives reached Wildcat territory only to fizzle out as frantic passes by the aerially inept Repton offense fell incomplete. Midway through the third quarter, Mackey, Stimpson and backup tailback Scott Norris drove the Wildcats deep into Repton territory, but Steele missed a thirty-seven-yard field goal attempt.

After taking a toss sweep and flying down the sideline for a long gain on the ensuing possession, Bulldog running back Mitchell Rankins came up limp and had to leave the game. Temporarily without their most potent offensive threat, another Repton drive died on the vine with four minutes remaining in the third. Rankins returned to the field after Sand Rock went three and out, but on the third down he fumbled the handoff. "That's about the fourth time we've put the ball on the ground, and we were fortunate to get it back," Johnson huffed from the press box as Repton's punter trotted onto the field once more.

The Wildcats made a mistake a short time later, fumbling inside their own twenty. Coach Rowe remembered the conversation he had on the sidelines as the Sand Rock defense huddled with their backs against the goal line. "Coach Jacoway looked at me and said, 'Oh, no. We're about to get beat,'" Rowe said. "But I looked out there, and the players were slapping each other and knocking each other around, getting motivated, and I looked back and told him there was no way we were going to let them score." For a moment, the young head coach had forgotten that his team, in Rowe's words, "could turn on their emotions whenever they wanted." A short time later, Jacoway's confidence was fully restored. On third and three from the fourteen, Norris busted through the Repton line, disrupting a handoff and causing another turnover.

By halftime, Jamie Pitts had spent two quarters trying to block Repton's monstrous defensive lineman and was mad as hell, mostly at himself. Pitts had gone into the locker room at halftime frustrated and dejected. "I told coach I couldn't block Dukes, and he told me he had known all week that there was no way I could block him. But they had never said that to me." Truth be told, Tommy Dukes was just about the only man Pitts had not been able to whip all year long. "That was the thing about it," Pitts said. "He wasn't really beating me, but I had never run up against anybody I couldn't beat." Sometime in the third quarter, Pitts and junior tackle Dan Andrews devised a strategy to slow down the towering defensive tackle. "I'd hit him high, and Dan would hit him low," Pitts said. "Then we'd swap it up every few plays so he'd never know who was going to hit him where."

The incessant pounding on the Bulldogs' star player finally took a toll. After chasing a bootlegging Lance Mackey around left end, Dukes was still lying on the ground clutching his ankle after the rest of the pile shuffled back to their huddles. His replacement on the defensive line was much less imposing, and the Sand Rock linemen quickly took advantage of someone a little closer to their own size. A few plays later, however, Dukes returned to the game and once again jerked Stimpson to a stop behind the line of scrimmage. Then, on third and seven, with everyone in the stadium expecting another off-tackle play to keep the clock running, Mackey took the snap from senior Clayton Robertson, stood straight up and fired a twenty-three-yard completion to Heard. "I was telling Mr. Johnson about that play at halftime," said a suddenly animated Teat. "I told him we hadn't used it, but that it worked pretty good last week. And it worked pretty good right then."

Mackey's next pass attempt—another strike down the middle toward Heard—did not work out so well, at least initially. A Repton player with a full head of steam grabbed the ball out of the air and bolted down the Wildcat sideline. Mackey quickly gave chase, wrapping his arms around the defender and yanking at the ball. When Mackey rolled over after making the tackle, the ball was lying on the ground right beside him. He fell on it just in front of a trailing official, who quickly signaled that Sand Rock had regained possession. Determined not to be responsible for any more early Christmas presents for the Bulldogs, Mackey soon found Whaley open for a fourteen-yard gain before Norris barreled through the line for a first down at the nineteen.

A short time before, after returning to the game following his ankle injury, Dukes had once again slammed Sand Rock's diminutive tailback to the ground. But this time, Dukes's long arms could not reach Stimpson, who scooted down to the four-yard line on a delayed draw. After Norris advanced the Wildcats to the two, Mackey stiff-armed a pair of Bulldogs, raced to the corner pylon and put the game out of reach, 14–6, with just under five minutes to play. Sand Rock's defense recovered the sixth Bulldog turnover less than three minutes later. After the offense returned to the field and Mackey took a knee for the final time, he looked up to see ten very familiar faces. Jacoway had made a point of getting all eleven of his seniors into the game so they could spend the last few seconds of their high school careers together on the field.

The senior class of 1986. *First row, left to right*: Mark Parker, Chris St. Clair, Jeff Whaley, Lance Mackey, Artie Mackey and Jim Tom Stimpson. *Second row, left to right*: Dewayne Heard, Dwain Boyd, Jamie Pitts, Clayton Robertson and Lyndon Tidwell. *Courtesy of Russell Jacoway.*

When the final seconds ticked off the clock, the mob of Sand Rock fans on the field became so dense that Pitts did not see any of his teammates until he made his way back into the locker room. Artie Mackey, who had pulled in the first big catch of the night and contributed several key stops on defense, will never forget what he witnessed when he eventually made his way back to the locker room. "Everyone was high-fiving," he said, "and people I'd never seen were hugging us, tears streaming down their faces." He saw something else that night that he had never witnessed before—his head coach moved almost to tears. "Coach Jacoway was trying to tell us how proud he was of us," Artie said. "He wasn't crying, but his eyes were glistening. It was pretty emotional."

As he sat in the bleachers watching a legion of proud Wildcat fans celebrate their team's first state championship, Cherokee County school superintendent Ed Arnold Jr. had every reason in the world to be proud of everyone associated with the Sand Rock football program, himself included. After all, twenty years before, he had been one of the driving forces behind the Wildcats' resurrection from the dead.

Chapter 2

THE BEGINNING

Anyone thinking of looking for Sand Rock on a map of Alabama should probably grab a magnifying glass first, lest frustration set in. Perhaps less exasperating would be to locate, in the northeast corner of the state, two significantly larger dots that identify the cities of Gadsden and Fort Payne. Those points are connected by the diagonal blue line that is Interstate 59, which runs roughly forty-five degrees from Gadsden on the lower left to Fort Payne on the upper right. Midway between the two cities and about fifteen miles due east is a thirty-thousand-acre man-made reservoir that splits Cherokee County right across the middle. Unless the search is being conducted on the proper type of map, it won't be obvious that there is an elevated area between I-59 and Weiss Lake, but the southern end of Lookout Mountain occupies that area.

For anyone unfamiliar with the local vernacular, perhaps some explanation of exactly what is considered a mountain in this part of the United States is in order. Lookout Mountain has a high point of only 2,300 feet above sea level and, technically, isn't a mountain at all. Rather, it is what geologists refer to as a big hill plateau. Without deteriorating into a full-blown geology lesson, Lookout Mountain is the most outwardly visible southern remnant of the Cumberland Plateau, which begins in northeastern Kentucky and slices across Tennessee before beginning to ebb as it enters Alabama and finally flattens out just northwest of Birmingham.

Any decent student of history would probably argue that the more interesting end of Lookout Mountain lies seventy miles to the northeast of Sand Rock, near Chattanooga, Tennessee. Located there is the sheer rock wall that a bunch of damned Yankees commanded by General Joseph Hooker had the audacity to scale to the very tiptop of in the fall of 1863, shooting every Johnny Reb they could find along the way. The "Battle Above the Clouds"—so named because the top half of the rise often becomes sheathed in fog when weather conditions are just right, as they were on that particular November 24—cost the Rebels over two thousand men, compared to only four hundred Union losses, and helped begin the free flow of supplies up and down the nearby Tennessee River that eventually opened the way for General Sherman's march to Atlanta. The northern end of Lookout Mountain is also home to the "View of Seven States" at Rock City (of barn and interstate billboard fame) and the steepest set of laid tracks in the world, the Incline Railway.

Still, the southern end of Lookout Mountain has qualities that make it unique and special to the people who call it home. Little River, the only waterway in the world that begins and ends atop a mountain, snakes through the area. Over the eons, the river's flow has formed the 600-foot-deep Little River Canyon and Grace's High Falls, the state's tallest at 133 feet. Somewhere up there, about an hour's drive southwest of the aforementioned landmarks, natural treasures and Civil War battlefields, is a four-way stop that marks the dead center of the tiny town of Sand Rock.

According to *The Heritage of Cherokee County, Alabama*, compiled in 1998 by the Cherokee County Public Library, early settlers to the area that is now Sand Rock came with plans to farm and eke out a simple living. Among the families listed as early inhabitants were the "Becks, Mitchells, Pearsons, Stimpsons, Helms, Parkers, Farmers, Clantons, Stowes, [and] Appletons." The compiled history explains how early settlers "developed the area by building churches, roads, a school and the necessary things to have a good community." Some time after the first few buildings were erected, "the Brindley brothers were passing through and stopped at a spring to get some water. One of them picked up a small stone and crushed it with his hands and it made sand. He said 'This is sand rock,' and since then the area has been known as Sand Rock."

Administrators took inspiration from other area high school teams, such as the 1931 Cherokee County Warriors (above), and instituted a football program at Sand Rock in 1939. *Courtesy of the Cherokee County Historical Museum.*

The 1952 Sand Rock Wildcats. The school changed its mascot from the Maroon Devils in the mid-1950s, about the same time the football program was eliminated in favor of baseball. *From the 1953 edition of the* Lookout.

In the early 1920s, local leaders, including prominent resident Dewey Broom, realized the need for a place to educate their children, so a junior high school was up and running by the end of the decade. "Later it became a high school with the first class graduating in 1932. The new high school brought many events to the community" and "along with the churches, became the backbone of the area."

Not surprisingly, given the existence of football programs in the nearby towns of Centre (since 1920), Collinsville (1921) and Cedar Bluff (1930), it was only a matter of time before the game caught on at Mr. Broom's institution of higher learning. According to the Alabama High School Football Historical Society, a group of young men from Sand Rock first took to the field in 1939. However, the society's website does not list any results until 1945, and the outcomes of the three games played that year—all losses, by a combined score of 126–0—set the tone for the next forty years. Sand Rock's first documented win did not come until November 1948, when they knocked off Walnut Grove by the score of 7–6. Sand Rock began each of the next five seasons with a different coach and managed only eleven more wins. In 1954, either because of the team's lack of success, the decision to focus on other sports such as basketball and baseball or because someone broke into the school and stole the team's uniforms and equipment (all have been mentioned as potential reasons by various sources), the football program was disbanded.

Whatever the reason for the suspension of football at Sand Rock, a decade later the team's previous lack of success had apparently been forgotten—or at least forgiven. A group of parents and teachers approached Ed Arnold Jr., then an assistant coach at Cedar Bluff High School, about rebuilding the program. During Arnold's six-year stint at Cedar Bluff under L.D. Bruce, the Tigers had gone 48-8-3. Bruce's '59, '61 and '62 teams had all finished their seasons undefeated, and all three—in the days before a state playoff system existed—had been named Class 1A state champions by the *Birmingham News*. If the football program was to be resurrected, folks in Sand Rock smartly figured that the best way to get started was by hiring a coach who already possessed a thorough understanding of what winning was all about.

Arnold, who had also played for Bruce before graduating in 1952, quickly jumped at the chance to direct a team of his own. "A group approached me and asked me if I was interested, and of course I was," he said. "I resigned my position at Cedar Bluff and made the change." Arnold said that when he first got to the school to evaluate what he had to work with, it didn't take long to realize there was only one piece of the puzzle in place—him. "When I got over there, we didn't have a piece of equipment, didn't even have a football field," Arnold said. "But the boys were ready for a program. At least, enough of them were."

Wendell Lawson, a star on the Sand Rock basketball team in the mid-1960s, remembered how he and several other students "got out and started begging money to get a [football] team started." Twenty years later, Lawson was a teacher at Sand Rock being interviewed by a newspaper reporter a few days before the '85 state championship game. He remembered how desperate he and his classmates had been for some Friday night lights on Lookout Mountain. "We wanted to play," he told the *Anniston Star*. "We got tired of hitchhiking to Collinsville and Centre to see football."

Everyone in north Alabama was familiar with the stellar basketball teams Sand Rock fielded year after year, so Arnold knew there was no shortage of athletes. Along with basketball coach Waymon Wester, Arnold and several members of the community quickly set about organizing a football program. First up was constructing a place to play.

"A lot of people helped us start the thing from scratch," Arnold said. "During the summer, we built a football field and sprigged it to try and get grass before fall." Local farmers drove their tractors to the school to plow up the baseball diamond and make room for a new home for the football Wildcats. Sammy Pate, the agriculture teacher, instructed members of the school's Future Farmers of America chapter to water the field regularly. "Sammy did a great job to help get the program off the ground," Arnold said. Whether the football equipment had been sold or stolen back in 1954 (or possibly burned in effigy), Arnold's next job was to acquire enough helmets, pads and uniforms to fill a locker room. "It was a lot of work, getting equipment together," he said. "The school and the community provided the money to get equipment. The principal, Mr. L.D. Pearson, was also very supportive." Before long,

Cedar Bluff assistant coach Ed Arnold Jr. was hired to revive the Sand Rock football program in 1965. *From the 1964 edition of the* Costa.

Arnold, Pearson and dedicated students like Lawson were able to scrape together enough money to purchase a set of brand-new maroon uniforms and shiny white helmets.

The next step for Arnold was to try and teach blocking and tackling to a bunch of boys who, over the course of a decade without a pigskin to toss around, had become much more proficient at fielding and dribbling. "We started trying to build, trying to get them familiar—of course, all young men would have been familiar with the general terms of football, that sort of thing," Arnold said. "It was just that they really didn't know much beyond that." The Alabama High School Football Historical Society lists the results of that first season as one win and six losses.

Arnold could not remember the particular circumstances of his first coaching victory in a season played so many years ago (the Wildcats defeated North Sand Mountain, 20–7, on their brand-new field), but he vividly remembered the circumstances surrounding his worst loss, a 45–0 thumping administered in Adairsville, Georgia. "I had graduated college with the coach there, and he said he needed a game and that we should come up and play them," Arnold said. The coach promised that he would take it easy on the inexperienced boys from Sand Rock and finally talked Arnold into making the trip. But when the Wildcats arrived, they were in for a surprise. "It just so happened [my friend] had had a gall bladder attack and had to have surgery," Arnold said. "The school's principal, an old former coach, coached that game in his place. He relived all his old memories that night, just wore us out."

At the end of the season, Bruce, who was also the principal at Cedar Bluff, gave up coaching in order to focus on his supervisory duties. So Arnold hauled his losing record back down Lookout Mountain and promptly went back to winning. Arnold coached two more seasons and improved his career win-loss record to 16-11, including two wins over Sand Rock by a combined score of 27–6.

Claude Hooper, an assistant coach at Sand Rock in the 1970s, said that Arnold was the right man for the job of getting the Wildcats going. "Because he knew football, and just because of who he was. He had a great personality," Hooper said. "Kids never having played football before, it could have been a disaster trying to start something like that. But he was able to organize, and teach those kids, and coach them in something they had never played before. It was a great disappointment when he left after that first year, but we all understood why."

The Sand Rock yearbook (whose title changed from the *Lookout* to the *Wildcat* in the mid-1950s) contains no photos, no scores and almost no mention of football before 1968. Apparently, the community at large was more excited about the return of the program than the students and teachers who chose how to fill the pages of the school's annual book of memories. Perhaps the explanation for the oversight can be found in the team's continued lack of success during the three years following Arnold's inaugural season. Sand Rock went through two more coaches and managed only four wins in thirty games from 1966 to 1968. The team's first winning record, which came one year later under another new head coach, finally got the attention of the yearbook staff.

Chapter 3

Things Can Only Get Better

Roy Knapp was already a well-known coach in Alabama by the time he took the job at Sand Rock the summer before the 1969 season. Over a career begun during the early years of World War II, Knapp had already proven his coaching prowess at Gaylesville, his alma mater, along with high schools in Dale, Washington and Choctaw Counties. His career record was a respectable 73-58-8 and included three consecutive eight-win seasons from 1950 to 1952. Knapp had also coached Gaylesville to its first win over Cedar Bluff in twenty-one years, a 13–0 victory in 1957. The following season, the sports staff at the *Birmingham News* voted Knapp's unbeaten Trojans the state champions in their classification. As sportswriter Jimmy Bryan pointed out in the May 14, 1961 issue of the *Gadsden Times*, just after Knapp announced he was leaving Gaylesville to take a coaching job at a new school in Tennessee, building successful football programs was practically the old man's specialty:

> *Big coaching assignments are nothing new to the little round man. He served as football coach at East Mississippi College before coming to Gaylesville to meet a challenge. Working with very limited personnel, Knapp has compiled an enviable record with his Trojan athletic teams. Included was a state Class "A" football championship in 1958 when the school fielded the only unbeaten team in its history.*

Eight years later, after coaching at high schools in Tennessee and Alabama, Knapp grabbed a whistle, headed back to his home county and went to work trying to turn around a fledgling football team atop Lookout Mountain.

Claude Hooper graduated from Sand Rock in 1965, just in time to watch the FFA boys begin trying to turn the school's baseball diamond into a football field during the summer before Ed Arnold Jr. resurrected the program. After a two-year stint as a helicopter crew chief in Vietnam, Hooper returned to Sand Rock and spent seven years as varsity basketball coach and assistant football coach. For five of those seasons he coached under Knapp and still has fond memories of the little fellow. "He was a good football coach, and he was good for Sand Rock at the time he was there." Hooper said that Knapp was "innovative," mostly because he was usually trying to figure out how to defeat more talented teams with his usual handful of hardworking, though generally smaller, Sand Rock boys.

Knapp had to be creative when he did not have a lot of players, which was practically every year. "We'd scrimmage the right side of the offense against the left side of the defense, things like that," Hooper said. "Lot of times us coaches would get out there with blocking dummies to simulate another player or two so our guys could get a look at what they were going to see on Friday. Still, a lot of times, they didn't really see what they were going up against until they got too into the game."

Hooper said that Knapp was a disciplinarian. Players and cheerleaders rode the same bus to away games, and there was absolutely no talking allowed on the ride to the other team's field. "If we won, everyone could talk on the way back," Hooper remembered. "But if we lost, no talking. Not one word. That was just one of his rules." Knapp also had a humorous side:

> *He was a comedian. We were playing Spring Garden, just getting our eyes drilled out. At halftime Coach Knapp goes over to one player and asks him why he isn't making any of his blocks. The kid says he's got two men on him. He goes to the next guy, who tells him, "Coach, I got two guys on me, too!" Same story from the third guy. Coach Knapp says, "Now I know why we're getting beat 20–0. Everybody's got two men on them. They're playing twenty-two men on defense!"*

Veteran coach Roy Knapp, a Gaylesville native, had the Wildcat football program headed in the right direction by the mid-1970s. In eight years at Sand Rock, Knapp compiled a record of 34-31-4. *From the 1970 edition of the* Wildcat.

If there was one knock Hooper had about the way Knapp ran the football program, it was his insistence on a light pre-game meal. "Before every game we went to the lunch room, where the ladies who worked there always prepared the same thing, according to Coach Knapp's orders," Hooper said. "We had a piece of toast, a boiled egg and a

Jack Green (leaning), who played football at the University of Alabama in the 1930s, watches from the sideline alongside fellow assistant coaches Claude Hooper (center) and James Rowe in 1972. *From the 1973 edition of the* Wildcat.

hamburger patty. That was it. Home or away, the first thing [Assistant Coach] Sammy Clanton and I always did right before kickoff was run to the concession stand and buy a hot dog."

Tommy McDaniel, a 1973 Sand Rock graduate who later became a member of the Cherokee County Board of Education, credited Knapp with creating a "big man on campus" mentality among his players, despite his own slight physical stature. "Before he was hired as head coach we had heard about Coach Knapp, and we thought he had mythical proportions, eight feet tall and four feet wide," McDaniel said. "But he was a smallish man. Still, we quickly learned to love him. He was great to play for and he worked hard and made believers out of us. He was a great motivator."

Although Knapp's overall record in seven years at Sand Rock was just above break-even (34-31-4), no one on Lookout Mountain was willing to look back on thirty years of disappointment and complain about twenty-two wins in his first four seasons and only one losing record (1-8 in 1974). By the time Knapp left Sand Rock after the '75 season, the football team was regularly featured as prominently as the basketball team in the pages of the *Wildcat*. More importantly, Knapp helped bring respectability and higher expectations to a football program that had never known how to do much of anything except lose. Perhaps because of the seeds Knapp planted at Sand Rock, generations of Wildcats fans who came along later did not know nearly as much about one-sided blowouts and losing seasons as their parents and grandparents. There were still a few bumps on the road to competing for a state championship, but one "little round man" definitely instilled a desire to achieve bigger and better things. What Sand Rock needed most after Knapp's departure was someone who could light a fire under the football team and keep it burning.

Chapter 4

MEN AT WORK

Between Roy Knapp's last day in the locker room at Sand Rock and Russell Jacoway's first, the football program sunk into a bit of a funk. From 1976 to 1980, the team went through two more coaches and won only fifteen games while losing thirty-four. In 1981, a tough-as-nails head coach named Jim Lowery gave the community its first-ever taste of success on the statewide level when the Wildcats went 10-2 and advanced to the second round of the playoffs. But the hard-driving Lowery did not exactly have a line of kids waiting outside his office door begging for a chance to play.

Jamie Pitts, a senior on the 1985 team, remembered what practice was like when he played for Lowery as a freshman. "One day he grabbed me by the facemask and asked me why I didn't just quit," Pitts said. "He did a lot of us that way, but I loved football, even though sometimes I felt stupid for being a glutton for punishment." Pitts might have been right to hate Lowery, but he was somehow drawn in instead. "I decided that SOB wasn't going to run me off," Pitts said with a grin. "I don't know if he earned my respect or demanded it, but he got it. He was tough on kids, a different kind of man. But he was still a good man."

Word of Lowery's extreme methods soon spread through the student body, and several potential players decided to skip the following season. As a result, Sand Rock's gridiron success was short-lived. In 1982, the Wildcats won their first game against Spring Garden and then dropped the next nine in a row. When Lowery turned in his resignation at the end of the school year to take a coaching job in Georgia, the athletic boosters frustratingly began their fourth coaching search in eight years, this time setting out to find someone they hoped would stay in Sand Rock long enough to make a difference. Perhaps whoever the new head coach turned out to be could find a way to win with a group of youngsters that no one else seemed able to keep pointed in the right direction for very long.

As it turned out, the athletic boosters did not have to look very far from home to find the right man. William Russell "Rusty" Jacoway Jr. grew up and attended school less than ten miles from the football stadium that today bears his name, in a town at the northwest base of the tail end of Lookout Mountain. Before construction of Interstate 59 in the early 1960s, U.S. Route 11 was the main road for automobiles headed north to Chattanooga or south toward New Orleans. Right alongside that vital artery, in the town of Collinsville, sat Jacoway's Motel. Somehow, amidst her duties as a housewife and mother of three, the former Nellie Sue Mince still managed to oversee the family business. Her husband, William Russell Jacoway Sr., worked in the body shop at a Ford dealership in Gadsden, twenty miles away.

The summer before Rusty began the eighth grade, his father had undergone surgery to repair a knee damaged years before in an auto accident. One morning a few months later, as Rusty was getting ready for school, his father suddenly felt ill and went into the bedroom to lie down. "Because of the way they did surgery back then, a blood clot had formed, and he had these attacks whenever it moved," Jacoway said. "That morning, the blood clot went to his heart and killed him." With his father gone and his older sister already away at college, Rusty quickly became the new man of the house to his mom and little brother. Luckily, Jacoway soon began receiving significant help in adjusting to his new roll from a fraternity he would eventually join.

Jacoway was a two-sport athlete at Collinsville High School, lettering in football three times and basketball twice. By his own admission, Russell Jacoway was far from most talented member of either team. "I started three years in football, but I was average at best," he said. "I might have started two basketball games my entire high school career." The fact that

Russell Jacoway lettered three years in football at Collinsville High School and was a member of the Panthers' 1975 state championship basketball team. *Courtesy of Russell Jacoway.*

he was not a starter on the basketball team did not lead to a rift between Jacoway and his coach. In fact, when Jacoway talks about the men for whom he played through the years who most influenced his career path, the name L.D. Dobbins is mentioned early and often. "He was as hard-nosed a basketball coach as I have ever seen. We did pushups on game day," Jacoway recalled. "We played one-on-one on game day at P.E. We shot foul shots, fifty a day, every day."

Also telling about the discipline and attention to detail that Dobbins instilled in his players was another drill Jacoway remembered well. "We learned to shoot lay-ups right- and left-handed," Jacoway said. "Coach Dobbins would stand under the goal, and if we didn't shoot them with good form, even if they went in, he would swat us with a broom. Hard." Despite the occasional whack on the back, Jacoway was not discouraged by such extreme coaching techniques. If future success is any indication, Jacoway already possessed the mentality he would need to emulate the success of mentors like Dobbins without resorting to their more extreme methods. He might not yet have fully recognized his inherent talent for teaching, but Jacoway already knew the desire to become a coach was there. "I had already been influenced by coaches like Steve Clay, who was my football coach at Collinsville, and I knew that was what I wanted to do for a living," Jacoway said. "By the eighth grade I was drawing plays instead of studying in class. By the ninth grade, I probably had my first playbook drawn."

Jacoway said that losing his father just as he was beginning to mature into a dedicated high school athlete often meant that the coaches for whom he played were the men he looked up to, both on and off the field. "Coaches had a lot of influence on me," he said. "There were several men around town who, after my daddy died, really kind of helped momma raise me. Not that she needed any help, but they kept an eye on me."

After graduating from high school, Jacoway attended community college before transferring to Auburn University. Once there, he regularly worked odd jobs to earn rent and spending money, somehow still managing to graduate in less than four years. "I was out of college and teaching by the time I was twenty-one years old," Jacoway said. He also got financial help from his mother along the way, though he said he still is not sure where the money came from. "My mother was not even a high school graduate, but she put three kids through college," he said. "All three of us graduated from Auburn. My mother managed that, and I'm still not really sure how she did it."

Jacoway said that he did not like it when his mother came to his basketball games because he was not very good and did not play often. "But she was at every football game I ever played," he said. Sadly, Jacoway's mother never saw her son become a head football coach. She died of cancer in October 1982 while Jacoway was still an assistant in southeast Alabama. In a day of starkly contrasting emotions, Jacoway's wife, Yvonne, gave birth to their first child on the day of his mother's funeral. Jacoway had to make the four-hour drive from a cemetery on Lookout Mountain to a hospital near Smiths Station in order to be there for his daughter's arrival, and he got there just in time. Jacoway

Russell Jacoway's parents, the former Nellie Sue Mince and Russell Jacoway Sr. Both passed away before their son began his head coaching career at Sand Rock in 1983. *Courtesy of Russell Jacoway.*

did not know it yet, but there was another long drive back to Cherokee County in his near future, one that would take place under much more pleasant circumstances.

Collinsville native Davis Norris had known Rusty Jacoway since his days as a volunteer with the town's youth baseball league. Norris had also followed Russell's career after college and was familiar with the promise he had already shown as an assistant football coach at high schools in Georgia and at Smiths Station, near Auburn. When Jim Lowery left Sand Rock, Norris knew that the football program could benefit from a coach with the type of dedication he had seen from Jacoway over the years. "Sand Rock had one year where they made the state playoffs, but the next year they were all the way back down again," Norris said. "They just didn't have much going for them."

Norris had coached against several of the current freshmen and sophomores a few years before when they participated in his baseball league in Collinsville, and he felt there was a wealth of talent about to come through the program. When Norris heard about Lowery's departure, he was convinced that Jacoway could be successful if he could get the job. "I told him if he was willing to go there and work and try to get the community back together—Sand Rock still just wanted to play basketball, for the most part—I told him they could be good if he could get the community behind him and if he was willing to stay a while," Norris said.

The choice came down to Jacoway and another coach. After Jacoway interviewed for the position, he spent the day at Norris's house awaiting word on which man the athletic boosters club planned to recommend to the local board of education, where all hiring decisions were made. In the end, Jacoway's promise to move his wife and daughter to Sand Rock—and, surprisingly, his ties to the head coach at his alma mater and Sand Rock's fiercest rival—probably helped him get the job. "Rusty came to the house on the day the board was going to meet and stayed most of the day at the house," Norris said. "Raymond Weaver, the football coach at Collinsville at the time, called some of the board members to try and help him get the job."

Coach Weaver may have helped Jacoway get hired, but he doubted that his new adversary would ever have any great success at Sand

Rock—and said so. "Weaver told him he'd like to see him get the job, but he didn't think he could win," Norris said. "Even Rusty's own brother told him he was crazy for taking the job."

Jacoway's wife, Yvonne, still remembers the circumstances that led to her life today in Sand Rock, as well as the consequences of a slight breach of etiquette that no one had told either of them to be sure to avoid. "Rusty had to interview with the whole athletic club, which was something we had never experienced before," she said. "Usually you just go talk to the superintendent or whoever is in charge of personnel. But he talked to the whole athletic club." Still, Yvonne said, Ed Arnold Jr.—the man who revived the football team in 1965 and had since been elected to run the entire county school system—was not happy that he had been excluded from the hiring process. "I remember when he got the job, Mr. Arnold crawled him up one side and down the other because he hadn't interviewed with him, personally," she said. "He just did what people told him to do, not realizing he had to go talk with Mr. Arnold before his hiring was made official."

Still, there was good news: The Jacoway family finally had a home. Well, sort of. Since the passing of Jacoway's mother, his younger brother had been trying to attend college classes while keeping the family business running. Russell and Yvonne temporarily relocated to Collinsville, living and helping out at the motel until it sold. "We actually stored all our furniture in a room in the back of the house and just lived in there, with furniture stacked floor-to-ceiling," Yvonne recalled. "When the motel sold later that winter, we moved out during a snow storm." The snow had already melted along the bottom of the mountain, but as is often the case when wintertime turns wet, the slope up and down Lookout Mountain was still quite slippery. "By the time we got to the top, the snow was still a foot deep," she said. "We would slide into the driveway, then the neighbors would push us out and we'd come back again with another load of furniture and slide in again." Finally, though, the Jacoways had some idea about their future, at least in the short term. Now, all Russell Jacoway had to do to make sure his high school sweetheart was not forced to load up and move again anytime soon was figure out a way to win a few football games.

In a state where everyone is identified and judged, at least initially, by the college team he or she roots for on Saturday afternoons, the two men charged with helping Jacoway turn around the football program at Sand Rock were just about as diverse as two Alabamians can be. James Rowe, an Auburn University graduate, had been a coach since 1970 and looked the part. Tall and lanky, with a casual gait that belied his true athletic intensity, Rowe had assisted Coach Roy Knapp for four years and then moved to another school before returning to Sand Rock in 1978. "I was re-hired at the same time as Sammy Clanton," Rowe said. "He was head football coach and I was head basketball coach, and we assisted each other because we were the only two coaches back then." When

James Rowe, an Auburn University graduate, began coaching in 1970 and served as Russell Jacoway's defensive coordinator for seven years. *From the 1986 edition of the* Wildcat.

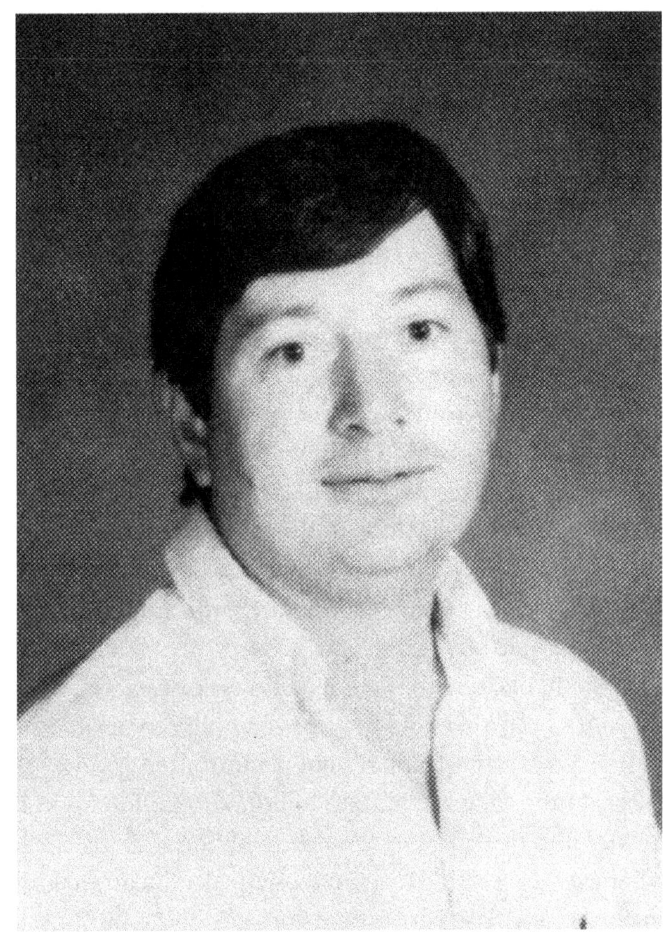

Roland Hendon, a University of Alabama graduate, was Jacoway's other assistant coach. From 1981 to 1986, Hendon also served as assistant principal and mathematics teacher at Sand Rock. *From the 1986 edition of the* Wildcat.

Jim Lowery replaced Clanton, Rowe became his assistant. After Lowery resigned, Rowe began preparing himself for the mental challenge of adapting his coaching methods to yet another new style and philosophy, whatever they turned out to be.

Roland Hendon was shorter and stockier than Rowe and looked more like a fullback than the quarterback he had once been in high school. A Crimson Tide supporter since long before he graduated from Tuscaloosa in early 1971 with a certificate in education administration, Hendon taught math and coached junior varsity football at Sand Rock. He, too, had experienced the ups and downs of the Lowery years and hoped that Sand Rock's next head coach could inspire more player participation and a level of consistency on the field that Hendon had not experienced since his hiring in 1981.

Rowe and Hendon both met twenty-five-year-old Russell Jacoway on the night he interviewed for the head coach's job, and neither was overly impressed. "I remember thinking he was pretty young," Rowe said. "I didn't really have an opinion of him, other than that." Hendon did not know what to think, either. "I'd never even heard of him, and I was concerned about how young he was," he said. "I had never worked for someone that young before." Jacoway remembered simply being grateful to have the experience of two men to draw from. "Since we're such a small school, I was glad to have them both," Jacoway said. "We played some schools back then that had one head coach and one assistant, and that was it." If Rowe and Hendon were uneasy about the whippersnapper who had just become their new boss, Jacoway was every bit as anxious. Would his new assistants cooperate with him and adhere to his coaching style, or would they fight him at every turn? "I knew I'd better get along with them, because they were all I was going to get," Jacoway said. "When they hired me, they told me I wasn't going to be able to hire anyone else."

Jim Lowery had not resigned until after spring practice, so Jacoway had no time to lose trying to build a football team in his own image. He moved into the office in the tiny field house along the home sideline and, whenever he wasn't teaching physical education to junior high school students, got down to the business of football. The handful of players Lowery hadn't run off would probably be back for the 1983 season, but Jacoway knew that he needed access to the talents of other athletes at the school who had steered clear of football.

Reaching out to the students, Jacoway scheduled a meeting and invited everyone. On the appointed day, several dozen boys filed into the gymnasium. The new coach began talking about working all year long, with a constant focus on football. Jacoway told the kids sitting in front of him that his players would eat the right foods, study their playbooks and lift weights year round. The speech impressed Hendon. "He really emphasized the weights, and that made all the difference in the world," Hendon said. "One of the most impressive things to me about the 1985 team was that we had kids who started out at the beginning of that season lifting with a certain weight, and at the end of the season they were lifting more weight. Usually you're going to wear down and not be as strong at the end of a season. That was amazing to me."

Jacoway also led by example. He put in long hours studying game film of his players to evaluate their talents and devised new strategies for upcoming opponents. "He was tireless," Hendon said. "I worked with four or five head coaches before I worked with Coach Jacoway and he, by far, put in more time and effort than any of the others." Jacoway's recruitment speech impressed the students, too. Instead of the slim number of players Lowery had been forced to work with during his tenure, Jacoway had over thirty players on his '83 team. Still, for anyone who measured coaching ability by wins and losses, Russell Jacoway's first season at Sand Rock was a total disaster.

Chapter 5

Heat of the Moment

By the time the Sand Rock Wildcats played their first game of the 1985 season, they were on the verge of completing an unbelievable turnaround. Two years before, the lowly Wildcats had rewarded their new head coach's commitment and dedication with ten mostly lopsided losses. The offense had been anemic, the defense more porous than a kitchen sponge. When the Wildcats lost their opener to the Spring Garden Panthers—a team even more hopeless, through the years, than Sand Rock—assistants James Rowe and Roland Hendon suspected they were in for a long season. Nine losses later, there were rumblings that the boosters might have recommended the wrong man for the job. "There were some questions and some skeptics, among both the players and the community," Hendon recalled. "There would be uncertainty anywhere, especially going 0-10 after being two years removed from the state playoffs." But Rowe and Hendon had definitely seen progress, even if it had been slow to show up between the hash marks on Friday nights. A year later, the team's improvement to 8-3, including a two-game run into the state playoffs, went a long way toward quieting most of the critics. "Coach Jacoway kept the team motivated, and that's always a hard job when the losses pile up," Rowe said. "Those two years kind of led to what happened in 1985."

Being a head coach's wife was something Yvonne Jacoway had spent years preparing herself for, but in 1983 those first ten losses took a mental toll. She was trying to get to know her new neighbors and find her family's niche in the community, but by the end of her first year on Lookout Mountain Yvonne's upstart husband hadn't achieved a darned thing, as far as the fans in the stands could tell. "I knew a few people, but that very first year it was tough being the person in the bleachers," she said. "Rusty's brother Jimmy was still here, and he was coming to the games. He would get fighting mad when they would start bad-mouthing the coach. It was hard to sit there and not say a word, but I'd tell him to keep quiet or we'd have a fight on our hands."

If Russell Jacoway ever sensed that his job was in danger, he must have felt a lot better after his first postseason boosters club meeting in late November 1983. "There had already been some talk about [firing me], and at that meeting there were several people there who didn't normally come." Jacoway said his first thought was that some of the new attendees might drum up enough support to get rid of him on the spot. "But instead of firing me that night, the boosters gave me three thousand dollars to buy helmets and other new equipment that we really needed. The officers

Russell Jacoway instructs seniors Dwain "Bubba" Boyd, Jim Tom Stimpson, Lance Mackey and Jeff Whaley during practice in the summer of 1985. *From the scrapbook of Jim Tom Stimpson.*

of the club at that time were extremely supportive." Jacoway said that he always believed his early benefactors realized that there wasn't exactly a wealth of talent to work with when he arrived at Sand Rock. And besides, no one else was clamoring for the job. "Vince Lombardi was not going to apply," he said.

By late August 1985, senior lineman Jamie Pitts was convinced that his third-year head coach was doing just fine. As a seventh grader, Pitts had begged his dad for the chance to go out for the junior varsity squad. "Daddy did not want me to play, but I bothered him so much that he got mad and told me to do whatever I wanted," Pitts said. As he progressed through high school, life at home became more complicated for Pitts. As

Jamie Pitts was an offensive lineman for the Wildcats in 1985. Even at five feet, eight inches and 135 pounds, he was still about the same size as most of the other linemen on the team. *From the scrapbook of Jim Tom Stimpson.*

a result, football gradually became much more than a pastime. "I had a lot of personal things I was dealing with in my life back then, and I guess nowadays kids with problems turn to drugs," Pitts said. "Football was my drug. I loved it more than anything else in my life. I had girlfriends back then, but if it came down to the guys wanting to watch film, or anything else related to football, I could have been right in the middle of having a kiss with a girl and I'd be, like, 'Gotta go!'"

After spending his freshman year as a tackling dummy on Jim Lowery's varsity squad, Jacoway moved Pitts from running back to guard. At five feet, eight inches and 135 pounds, Pitts certainly did not look like he ought to be wearing jersey no. 50. Then again, he was the same size as most of the other offensive linemen on the team. Another plus for Pitts was that ever since Jacoway's arrival, he no longer had to pour his battered body out of bed every morning. By all accounts Jacoway was a tough coach, but he did not believe in ordering his players to viciously pound on one another all day, every day. The "bullpen" tackling exercise Lowery had once employed to instill toughness was first to go. "That drill would probably be illegal today," Pitts laughed. "You'd just go and go and go at each other. Once you couldn't get up any more, your buddy—if he was any buddy to you at all—would reach down, grab you by the jersey and get you out of the way so you wouldn't get hit again."

Instead of being battered and bruised, Jacoway wanted his players stronger and smarter. Suddenly, drills that left players too tired to lift their arms, or in too much pain to concentrate on blocking assignments, were no longer considered to be the most desirable training methods. "When I first started practicing under Coach Jacoway, I didn't feel like I had practiced at all," Pitts said. "Suddenly, it wasn't about pain all the time, or about fighting and trying to kill each other." By redefining the work ethic, Jacoway had also restored something the Wildcats had been missing for as long as Pitts could remember—respect. "For years it was, like, if you play Sand Rock, you're going to get in a fight. The football team really had a bad reputation," Pitts said. "Coach Jacoway turned all of that around." Now, instead of nursing injuries every night after practice, Pitts found himself immersed in the mental aspects of the game. "He gave us playbooks and told us to study them and learn them," Pitts said. "Lots of times when I had homework to do I'd grab that playbook instead and read until I fell asleep."

There must have been a page missing from the playbook Pitts was reading the night before the season opener against Spring Garden. While covering a punt in the first half, Pitts made a stupid mistake, or so his head coach thought and indicated to him—loudly and repeatedly. Pitts admitted that he "wasn't really thinking" when the Panthers' punter kicked the ball almost straight up in the air. "I was going to catch the ball and run with it," Pitts said. "Wrong thing to do. The ball came down and I was right in the middle of a mess. I touched the ball, and then someone nailed me right in the stomach." Sand Rock overcame the error and went on to win the game handily, but after that bonehead play the head coach had a bone to pick with Pitts, and there was nowhere to hide. "Once the game starts, you tune out everything except what you know you have to do. It's like tunnel vision," Pitts said. "All the sudden I snapped out of it, because all I could hear was Coach Jacoway screaming at me." Pitts tried to slink away and started edging down the sideline. "But as I moved away, he just ran with me," Pitts said. "He was screaming at me and then he whacked me on the back of the helmet. I lost my tunnel vision for a minute or two."

Pitts eventually got his vision back, and ended up making the play of his life. With the Wildcats up 31–0 early in the fourth quarter, another errant football came floating toward Pitts, who had gone into the game at the linebacker position. Spring Garden's offense had driven all the way down to the two-yard line when their quarterback dropped back to pass. "Then someone hit him," Pitts said. "The ball went straight up in the air, and I caught it and went all the way for a touchdown." Even after covering ninety-eight yards and tying a school record, all Pitts could think about was the tongue-lashing he had received in the first half. "I was still upset at myself about getting chewed out," Pitts said. "I took my helmet off and moped back over to the sideline. About that time, Coach Jacoway yelled at me again. He said, 'Cheer up Pitts, you just scored a touchdown!' I had gone from zero to hero—literally."

There were plenty of heroes by the time the game ended with the score 38–8. Lambasted by his coach early on, Pitts had bounced back to finish the game on a high note. Among the first teammates to slap Pitts on the back after he reached the end zone was his good friend, Jeff Whaley, who had run escort all the way down the field during the interception return.

Whaley had just played the game of his life, too. The senior had scored touchdowns on two long passes and returned a punt fifty-nine yards for another. As Pitts and Whaley celebrated with their teammates on the bus ride home, neither could have foreseen that the next game would provide Whaley with a chance to slip up. Unlike Pitts, however, Jeff Whaley waited until there was no time left on the clock before making one of the most crucial mistakes of the entire season.

Chapter 6

WORKING OVERTIME

Sand Rock's second game of 1985 took place on September 5, exactly thirty days after the official start of summer practice. Of course, the football team had already been participating in Coach Jacoway's off-season program for months. Players were expected to attend a minimum number of weightlifting sessions, and extensive conditioning was recommended, if not entirely mandatory, well before helmets started crashing. "We did bust the weights," Jim Tom Stimpson said. "And I remember running when I didn't have to." There were always a few players who either did not or could not participate in the required number of summer workouts, and since there was no running track on the Sand Rock campus, punishment for absences was administered via laps around both goal posts. In a show of solidarity, Stimpson, along with several other players, ended every practice by running all the combined laps their teammates had accumulated.

The Wildcats were determined to be in better shape than their opponents. They also wanted to be stronger. Sand Rock's weightlifting program was more comprehensive than most high schools in northeast Alabama at the time, though the equipment hardly reflected the advantage. Homemade barbells and dumbbells in the makeshift workout room had been constructed from metal plates cut with an acetylene torch and then welded to metal rods. As a result, players could not add or subtract plates to change the total weight. They either lifted the 211-pound barbell or the 247-pound barbell—there was nothing in between. "Olympic equipment was scarce," Stimpson recalled.

Still, Jacoway frequently awarded T-shirts with the words "225-lb. Club" or "250-lb. Club" as players grew stronger and advanced from one oddball lifting station to the next. On the practice field, players enhanced their leg strength with another unorthodox apparatus straight out of the junkyard. "I remember we had these eighteen-wheeler tires," Stimpson said. "We had to strap on a harness and pull them, running back and forth." Stimpson credited the pulling of tires for helping him gain over 1,200 yards on the ground in 1985. "But I didn't like them at the time, not even a little bit."

Practices were fairly typical. After getting into their pads, players lined up for stretching exercises. Then they split into groups for specialized instruction: Jacoway was in charge of quarterbacks and running backs, assistant Roland Hendon took tight ends and receivers and defensive coordinator James Rowe coached the linemen. Backs worked on their timing in the backfield, ends and flankers ran pass patterns and linemen learned to stay low by hitting the chutes. Monday was reserved for film study and conditioning; Thursday was typically spent in helmets and shorts, fine-tuning the game plan for the next opponent. The really hard work, conducted in full pads, took place on Tuesday and Wednesday. "They were a special group of kids because they loved to hit each other," Rowe said. "They hit each other harder than they hit the other team, and that made practice fun." Rowe said that the players did not always get along off the field, and sometimes not even on the practice field. "But during the ballgames they were always together," he said. "There were no troublemakers, they were just boys. Good boys."

Every week, Jacoway fine-tuned his offensive and defensive playbooks in order to take advantage of weaknesses he and Rowe had detected during their weekend film study sessions. After he decided on a plan of attack for the week, Jacoway jotted down a page or two of plays that he felt would be most effective, along with motivational notes and the occasional humorous quotation. "As much as anything, I wrote all that out just to get my thoughts together," he said. "I used those notes at practice, and if it wasn't in there we didn't run it." Every Monday, Jacoway delivered mimeographed copies of his backward-stapled packets (he is left-handed,

J. T Stimpson

SANDROCK Wildcats

1985

Contenders

or

Pretenders

The Panthers want

You!

This page and next: Russell Jacoway's typical weekly play packet was composed of plays designed for the upcoming opponent and typically featured a motivational slogan on the cover sheet. (Note the staple in the upper-right corner.) *From the scrapbook of Jim Tom Stimpson.*

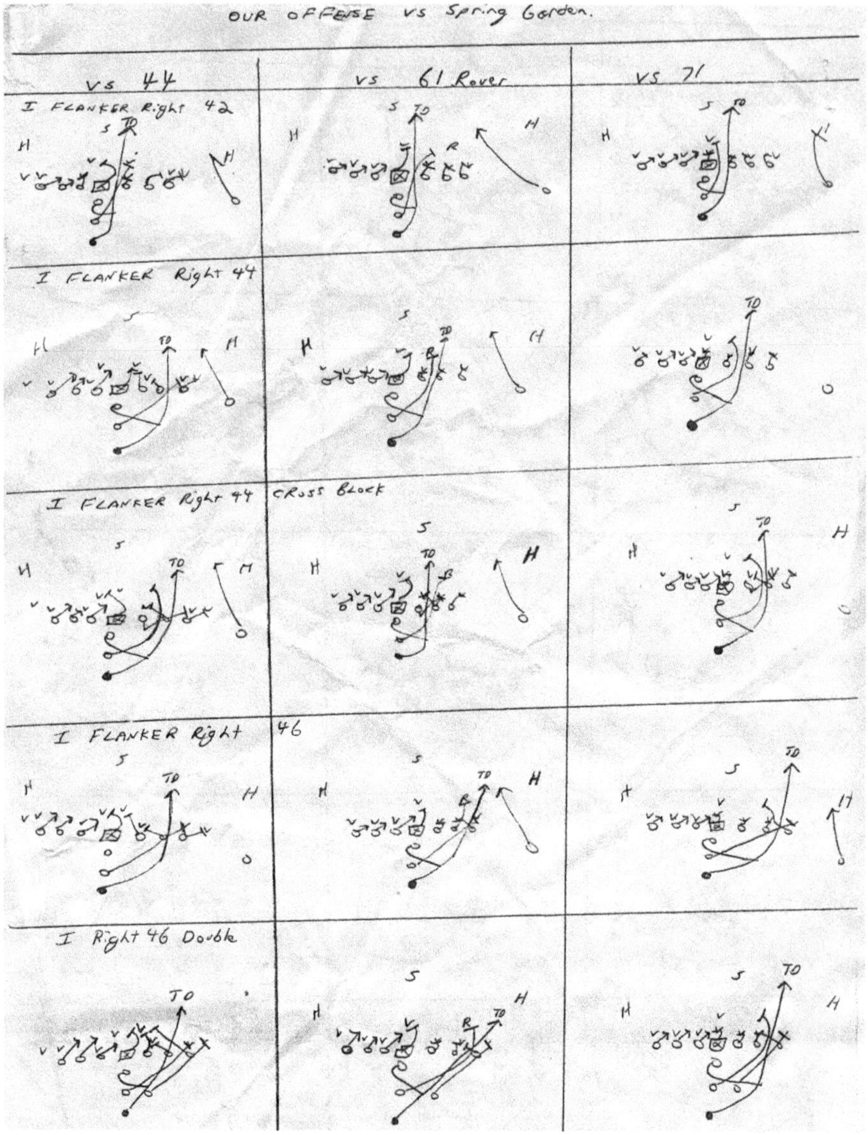

OUR OFFENSE vs Spring Garden.

vs 44	vs 61 Rover	vs 71
I FLANKER Right 42		
I FLANKER Right 44		
I FLANKER Right 44	CROSS BLOCK	
I FLANKER Right	46	
I Right 46 Double		

which meant the staple usually landed in the upper-right corner) to the players. No copies survive of Jacoway's thoughts for the week two game against Cedar Bluff, but the week one handout, which reminded players not to "look past" Spring Garden, offers a hint at the seriousness with which the Sand Rock coaching staff approached their most imposing Area 16 opponent. The concern was reasonable, because Sand Rock's rivalry with Cedar Bluff had been lopsided for years. The Tigers had won seven in a row beginning in 1977 and nine of the last eleven. In 1984, Jacoway's boys had finally snapped the streak with a 14–6 win at home. Now, the young head coach was about to bus his Wildcats back down the mountain to L.D. Bruce Field, where he knew he would get the very best the revenge-minded Tigers had to give.

As was common practice at the time, coaches at smaller schools often scheduled the first game or two of the season for Thursday night. By the end of August, everyone in northeast Alabama was more than ready for football to begin, and tweaking the schedule was a great way to sell more tickets and peddle a few extra soft drinks to eager fans with nothing better to do until Friday night rolled around. As a result of that scheduling decision, the bleachers were packed well before the 7:30 p.m. kickoff, the crowd expecting a game that figured to go down to the wire—or possibly even into overtime.

Unlike Sand Rock, which featured a solid team of steady performers, Cedar Bluff had the closest thing to a superstar anyone at either school had seen in years. Senior David Blevins had received wide acclaim the year before after rushing for well over a thousand yards and nearly twenty touchdowns. Blevins's classmate, Tony Crane, had blocked for him on offense from the fullback spot and then swapped to linebacker on the change of possession. Crane's play on defense had earned him postseason honors in 1984, as well. A quarter-century later, Jeff Whaley still remembered his initial impression from crossing paths with Cedar Bluff's two best players. "Nobody hit me harder, all year long, than David Blevins and Tony Crane," Whaley said. "Nobody."

Of the seven *Gadsden Times* sportswriters who participated in the paper's weekly "Pigskin Pick 'Em" feature that week, five had forecast a Sand Rock victory. Sports editor John Alred, in his weekly column, predicted a 14–7 Wildcat win. Just about everyone, it seemed, was figuring on a defensive struggle—and they got one that people still talk about today.

Sand Rock fumbled the opening kickoff, handing the Tigers an excellent scoring opportunity at the twenty-five-yard line. But the Wildcat defense held firm throughout the first quarter, and neither team threatened again until Sand Rock drove to the Tiger thirteen-yard line late in the second. On fourth down, kicker Tommy Steele missed a thirty-yard field goal attempt, but a Cedar Bluff player crashed into his leg during the follow-through, and Sand Rock got four more tries at the end zone. This time, it was the Tigers' defense that rose to the challenge. On fourth and goal from the one, Crane and a host of other Tigers slammed quarterback Lance Mackey to the ground just short of the goal line as the first-half clock expired. In the third quarter, the defenses again lived up to pre-game expectations, with each forcing a pair of turnovers. In the fourth quarter, each team got close enough to try game-winning field goals, but Steele missed a thirty-five-yarder, and Cedar Bluff's try from thirty-two yards sailed wide right as the clock expired on a scoreboard filled with zeroes.

Overtime in Alabama high school football is fairly simple and works as follows: After a coin toss to determine possession, both teams get a turn at the end zone from the ten-yard line. If the first team kicks a field goal, for example, the second team breaks the huddle knowing it can win the game with a touchdown or force a second overtime with a field goal of its own. Teams take turns until someone wins.

Cedar Bluff won the toss, already having played the game of a lifetime against the number three–ranked team in the state. Suddenly, however, the Tigers seemed determined to hand their most hated rival an easy win. On first down, Blevins barreled down to the 1-yard line, but a clipping penalty backed the ball back past the 20. On first and long, another penalty pushed the ball to the 40-yard line. Suddenly, it was third and goal from near midfield in overtime of a game in which the Tigers had produced only 139 yards of offense, all on the ground. If there was one thing Cedar Bluff did not do well, it was throw the football. As a result, just about everyone in the Tigers' huddle was resigned to the distinct possibility of losing when the play call came in from the sideline: a fake-toss-sweep-Hail-Mary pass that hardly ever worked at practice.

The Tigers were not the only players on the field who were surprised by the call. Jeff Whaley, who had played expertly against Spring Garden the week before, was in his usual spot on defense at deep safety. It was his job to make sure no receiver got behind him and that no passes—especially those flung as far as possible in the last-ditch hope for an absolute miracle—were caught in his area of the field, which was pretty much everywhere between the linebackers' butts and the goal line. The following morning, the *Gadsden Times* reported that it was Vince Shedrick who caught the forty-yard bomb from Blevins that gave the Tigers their first lead of the night (and the Wildcats their only deficit of the entire season). But Whaley knew that report was not accurate. "I was the one who let Harrell Horton get behind me," he said. "I was the safety. That was me." The Tigers were so excited to be in the lead that the hastily kicked extra point fell short. Still, Cedar Bluff had the lead, 6–0. All their defense had to do now was the same thing it had done all night: keep the Sand Rock offense out of the end zone.

Over on the Wildcat sideline, Whaley was beside himself. He had blown his assignment on a pass that should never have been completed, and now his teammates were going to have to save his backside or the

Senior flanker Jeff Whaley was one of the Wildcats' go-to receivers in 1985, but his missed assignment against Cedar Bluff in week two almost cost Sand Rock its first undefeated season. *From the 1986 edition of the* Wildcat.

Wildcats would be 1-1 and no longer ranked number three—and those would be the least of their troubles. With an Area 16 loss so early in the season, Sand Rock would have to fight it out with Gaylesville, Spring Garden and defending state champion Valley Head for the second and final spot in the playoffs. Whaley wished for a way to make up for his mistake. Maybe Coach Jacoway would call for a pass to him, he thought, or maybe they would run the ball his way. Whaley was definitely mad enough to flatten anyone who lined up across from him.

After an offside penalty on first down moved the ball to the five-yard line, Whaley got the chance he had been craving. As he leaned into the huddle and listened to the play call, Whaley knew he was about to get one last shot at redemption. The play Jacoway sent in was a handoff to Dwain "Bubba" Boyd toward the right, Whaley's side. He looked up at his fullback and told him not to worry about the linebacker. "Just come on," Whaley said. "He's all mine." After Boyd bounded into the end zone behind Whaley's block, Tommy Steele's point-after kick split the uprights, and hundreds of happy Wildcat fans screamed from the bleachers. Still, no one in Cherokee County was as overjoyed as Jeff Whaley. "I have never in my life been so grateful for somebody to pull me out of a hole," he said. "I knew I would have been the one to carry that around from then on, that I was the one who let them score."

As he trotted from the sideline toward the middle of the field to celebrate with his players, Assistant Coach Roland Hendon sensed that such a dramatic victory over a team as talented as the Tigers could be the start of something special. "[Cedar Bluff] had been tough for several years, and just knowing that we could beat them, that helped a lot," Hendon said. "That win probably propelled us more than anything."

If the Wildcats had any serious aspirations about propelling themselves into the state playoffs, they were going to have to find a way to slip past another pack of Tigers in week three. Unfortunately, they had never enjoyed a great deal of success against the team from Valley Head. In fact, Sand Rock had only defeated the defending state champions twice in the previous thirty-eight years.

Chapter 7

Kicking in the Door

After the thrilling overtime win over Cedar Bluff in week two, Russell Jacoway and his assistants were rewarded with the unenviable task of trying to figure out a way to beat the defending state champions. Valley Head had already gotten off to a slow start at 0-2, but the Tigers had begun the season ranked number two in Class 1A. The game would also be a rematch of the second-round playoff game from the year before. Largely because of that distinction, a win over the defending state champs—especially a convincing one—would still turn heads all across Alabama.

At least the Wildcats had Valley Head at home this time. The year before, Sand Rock had taken a pounding on the road, the 48–7 loss reminding coaches, players and fans alike how it felt to be humiliated. What was worse, during the game Sand Rock had been penalized repeatedly for arguing with both their opponents *and* the officials. In fact, several players from both teams ended up watching from the sidelines after being tossed out for fighting. It had been a sorry spectacle, tremendously embarrassing—especially to Jacoway. For forty-five minutes, the young coach had presided over a "come to Jesus" meeting in the post-game locker room. (Actually, the dressing-down took place in the Valley Head Volunteer Fire Department, which doubled as the visiting team's dressing area.) Jacoway made it clear that his players did not fight, cuss or mouth off to anyone. Play with class, he told them repeatedly. To drive home the point and serve as their penance, players jogged lap after lap after lap around the goal posts at the next practice. The Wildcats took Jacoway's sermon to heart, winning six of their next seven games in '84 with style and grace, including an opening-round playoff win on the road that produced a rematch with Valley Head. And at least one person who played in that game still believes that the Wildcats would have won it if only the darned quarterback had run the ball instead of trying to throw it.

Lance Mackey had been playing football at Sand Rock since the first year he was eligible to go out for the junior varsity squad. Like most seventh graders at the time, Mackey had grown up watching and listening as Paul "Bear" Bryant's Alabama Crimson Tide teams won consecutive Southeastern Conference championships and multiple national titles. Perhaps because of those experiences, Mackey, an all-around athlete, loved football more than all the other sports at which he excelled. Lance's father, Bud, never got the chance to go out for football at Sand Rock—he had been a student during the eleven-year lull in the program during the late 1950s and early '60s. But he was entirely behind his son's efforts to shine on the gridiron. Lance's mother, however, was another story. "The coaches wanted me to go out for varsity even in the eighth grade and my mom said no," Lance Mackey said. "I did in ninth grade, but she was still scared to death."

Mackey had begun his playing career as a tight end. By his second year on the junior varsity, in 1981, someone suggested he try out for quarterback. Jim Lowery liked the way Mackey handled the ball in the backfield, so he played the position for the entire season. The following year, perhaps because of the shortage of players Lowery had become famous for producing with his brutal training techniques, Mackey got a new position and a new number. "I started out as an offensive guard, but after one game they figured out I wasn't very good at blocking anybody," Mackey chuckled. "I wore no. 61." But he played lineman like a zero, so the coaches repossessed his jersey and moved him back to quarterback. In Lowery's final season at Sand Rock, Mackey watched from behind center as Wildcat running backs ran into wall after wall of defenders on the way to losing nine in a row.

By the end of the 1983 season, Jacoway had added another ten games to Mackey's personal losing streak, and the failed offensive lineman was drained from dealing with the disappointment. Following a 21–0 loss to North Sand Mountain midway through the schedule, Mackey decided that it was time for someone else to bash his head against the wall. "I had been quarterback for a year and a half, and we had lost every game I started," Mackey said. "I guess you just get to an emotional point sometimes where you just break down. That game was mine." Through the angry tears in his eyes, Mackey told Jacoway that he was tired of losing and suggested he find someone else to run the offense. Mackey said that he would do whatever it took, play whatever position necessary, to turn around the team's fortunes and flush away the sick feeling that seemed to coat his stomach every Saturday morning. Mackey told Jacoway that if winning meant someone else ought to be the quarterback, then that was fine with him.

Young as he was, Jacoway was still wise enough to envision a future that Mackey could never have imagined as he sat alone in the locker room with his head in his hands. "He could see, as an adult, that we were going to be better," Mackey said. "He encouraged me, told me not to give up, said everything was going to be fine." But despite the much-improved play of an emotionally rejuvenated Mackey over the final four games of '83, the wins still didn't come. As a result, Mackey knew that *everything* was going to have to get *fine* pretty fast, or he and his teammates might find themselves learning football out of someone else's playbook. "I remember somebody telling me before our junior year [1984] that Coach Jacoway was going to have to turn it around or he was going to be gone," Mackey said. "I remember it really sinking in with me that we needed to do something, because I liked him and didn't want to start my senior year with another new coach."

By the fall of 1984, the Wildcats had done *something*, indeed. Jacoway and his two-man staff had turned the 0-10 Wildcats into an 8-2 playoff team. Still, defensive coordinator James Rowe shook his head in disgust every time he thought about the drubbing his defense had suffered at Valley Head in week three. The Tigers' offense had been as predictable as a freight train—and every bit as unstoppable. Sand Rock's best eleven defenders were tiny compared to the starting Valley Head halfbacks and did little to slow them down. Faced with the prospect of another lopsided defeat in the playoffs, Jacoway and Rowe began looking for a friend in the coaching world who could loan them a workable plan for stopping the Valley Head wishbone. If they did not borrow someone's defensive scheme and install it in time for Friday night, both coaches feared that the Wildcats were destined to end yet another season with a bitter taste in their mouths, eight-win season or not.

Jacoway and Rowe had a legitimate coaching emergency, so there is little irony in the fact that they settled on a scheme someone else had already dubbed "mayday." "I had seen the defense run before, it was a blitzing 4-4," Rowe said. "Bobby Joe Johnson and Bobby Beckett, the coaches over at Centre, had used 'mayday' whenever they felt they were outmanned," Jacoway said. "Well, we knew we were outmanned, so we tried it." On Friday night, Rowe kept his defensive unit in the desperation formation for almost the entire game, a coaching strategy that worried Jacoway immensely even though he knew it was the Wildcats' best shot to win. "He kept saying, 'They're going to throw it,'" Rowe said. "They'd send twin receivers to one side, but I'd stay in that defense. We came after them, sent at least six guys on just about every play." Beside him on the sideline, Jacoway bit his tongue and let Rowe call the game as he saw fit.

For most of the night it appeared that "mayday" was going to save the day. It almost did. Valley Head lacked the talent to put the ball in the air, and Sand Rock actually held the lead late in the game before the Tigers put together a go-ahead touchdown drive. The Wildcats quickly drove back down the field and scored another touchdown, pulling to within one point with fifty-six seconds remaining. As Sand Rock fans screamed coaching suggestions from the grandstands, Jacoway called timeout and trotted onto the field; he already knew that he was not going to play for the tie. Several times during the week, fans and fellow coaches had congratulated Jacoway for the Wildcats' unbelievable turnaround and then lamented their impending loss to a team that almost everyone had already crowned as state champions. "Not so fast, armchair quarterbacks," Jacoway might have thought as he and his players gathered on the ten-yard line with a chance to win a game that almost everyone in the bleachers had given away days before.

Actually, Jacoway was thinking how thankful he was that, despite being thoroughly outmatched, his players had somehow managed to keep within striking distance of Valley Head for four quarters. Jacoway felt

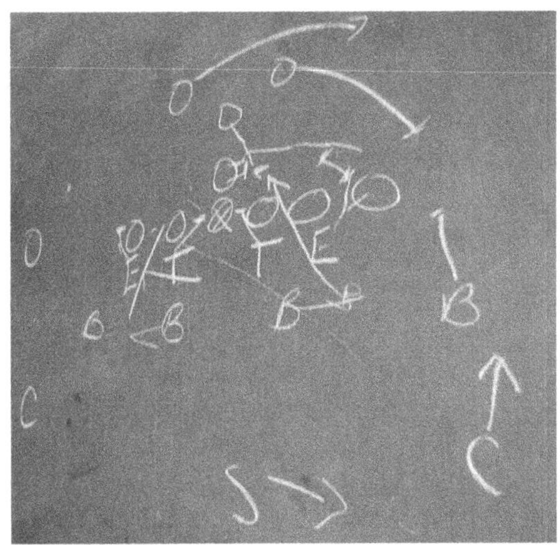

Sand Rock's borrowed defense, known as "mayday." The Wildcats successfully employed the blitzing 4-4 scheme against Valley Head in the 1984 state playoffs. *Illustration by James Rowe.*

certain that the Wildcats were down to their last chance now, though, and he wanted this one to be over sooner rather than later. "If we had tied that game and gone into overtime, we could not have beaten them from the ten-yard line," Jacoway said. "They were a very physical football team." So instead of kicking the extra point, Jacoway decided to try for the two-point conversion with a delay pass to the halfback. It was the same play that had worked for the touchdown on the previous play, only to the opposite side. At the snap, helmets crashed and bodies flew. Lance Mackey can still see the play in his mind as it unfolds: No. 12 takes the snap, rolls out to the right, lobs a pass over a defender's head and watches as the ball floats…floats…floats, just over the extended fingertips of the intended receiver. "If I could go back and change one thing, I would go back and run that ball," Mackey said. "There was nobody around. All I had to do was run the ball."

Instead, the football fluttered to the turf. That's all, folks. Turn out the lights. Cue the fat lady. Party over. Valley Head wins, 17–16, and three weeks later the Tigers fulfilled everyone's expectations by winning the state championship. Sand Rock fans who had been entirely behind the two-point try a few seconds earlier suddenly began to openly question the head coach's mental ability. "The same folks who had been yelling to go for the win were suddenly wondering what the heck I was thinking," Jacoway remembered. "To this day, I would not change that call." The

Quarterback Lance Mackey overcame two years of growing pains to become the undisputed leader of the Sand Rock football team in 1985. *From the 1986 edition of the* Wildcat.

coaching staff had been deeply concerned that a second trouncing by Valley Head might destroy the team's psyche for the entire off-season. Instead, Jacoway, Rowe and Hendon had employed an unconventional defensive approach that solidified the Wildcats' confidence in their coaches and themselves *despite* a heartbreaking loss in the state playoffs.

"After [Valley Head] went on to win it all, our kids said that if they could come that close to beating the eventual state champion, they could win it all the next year," Rowe said. A few days later, as they turned in equipment and cleaned out their lockers, players noticed a message Coach Jacoway had written on the blackboard: "This year we knocked on the door. Next year, we're kicking it in!" By the end of the Valley Head game the following year, the Wildcats had certainly kicked in the proverbial door. They had also ripped it off its hinges and used it to repeatedly belt the Tigers in the tail.

Valley Head had begun the 1985 season ranked number two in Class 1A, but by the time they traveled to Sand Rock on September 13, the Tigers were halfway through a season-opening five-game losing streak. Both starting halfbacks from the year before had graduated. Needless to say, the team's top-ten ranking was long gone, too. Still, none of the Wildcats minded that they had to settle for being the third team to whip the defending champs. They owed Valley Head a licking for a multitude of indiscretions dating back to 1947, so they made sure to give them a good one.

During his sophomore year, Lance Mackey had come to hate playing in the Wildcats' close losses even more than in the more lopsided defeats. "When you lose that many games, you just don't want to do it anymore," he remembered. "It's such a bad feeling." With those memories in mind, Mackey did everything he could to make sure the Valley Head game was not close. The year before, Mackey had thrown a pass when he felt he should have run. This time he did plenty of both, just to be safe. Mackey scored the game's first touchdown on a 2-yard keeper, and finished with 215 passing yards and three touchdowns—one each to seniors Jeff Whaley, Dwain "Bubba" Boyd and Dewayne Heard. The final score was 49–6.

Two years earlier, Lance Mackey's mother had sat in the bleachers on Friday nights and listened as the crowd shouted toward the sidelines, calling her son's efforts pitiful and lamenting that the poor kid simply did not know how to get the job done. At the exact same time, Russell Jacoway had seen something completely different: desire, effort and a level of ability that would, with experience and positive feedback, grow into an indestructible desire to win. By the end of the Valley Head game, Mackey was an experienced senior and the undisputed leader of the Sand Rock Wildcats. He eventually came to realize that the past disappointments he and his teammates had suffered were just as important in their overall development as the successes that followed. "I think us losing nineteen games in a row had as much to do with us winning the state championship as anything," Mackey said years later.

In the late summer of '85, though, a much younger Lance Mackey had not yet won his final fifteen games as a starting quarterback and so did not look on the losses with the gratitude he does today. The only

Lance Mackey finished his senior season with over fourteen hundred passing yards and another five hundred yards rushing. He was named the Class 1A Player of the Year in 1985. *From the scrapbook of Dan Andrews.*

thought about losing that lingered in the back of his mind at the time was that he had already had his fill of that dish and wanted it banished from the menu. Luckily for Mackey and the rest of the Wildcats, most of what was left of the regular season turned out to be a piece of cake.

Chapter 8

TAKING WHAT THEY'RE GIVING

In week four, Lance Mackey lit up the scoreboard early and often against White Plains in a game that Sand Rock went on to win 35–0. Two touchdown passes to Jeff Whaley covered over one hundred yards and accounted for all the points scored in the first half. In the third quarter, Mackey tossed another score to Dewayne Heard. A few minutes before completing that pass, Mackey had handed off to the team's starting tailback for a one-yard plunge that ran the score to 20–0. The ball carrier was a young man who always made the most of every moment he spent on the football field, despite the fact that he sometimes seemed intent on frittering away the majority of time he spent off it.

In the fall of 1985, Jim Tom Stimpson was one heck of a running back, if not much of a role model. If you don't believe how much of an inspiration he was *not*, just ask him. "Back then, I was very much a punk," Stimpson said. "I was the kind of kid who, when no one was looking in the classroom, the spitball or obnoxious noise was quite possibly my doing." Still, Stimpson applied himself well enough to make good grades. His parents rewarded his scholastic achievements with a brand-new Camaro just in time for senior year, and the school invited him to join the Beta Club. He might not have been the biggest or strongest kid in his class, but Stimpson was always among the quickest. His slight frame meant that a certain amount of agility came naturally, and he further sharpened his abilities in elementary school by playing dodge ball and pretending to be

Jim Tom Stimpson (34) was not big or strong, but the shifty tailback rushed for over 1,200 yards in 1985. *From the scrapbook of Jim Tom Stimpson.*

the title character from the hit 1970s TV show *The Six Million Dollar Man*. When he turned seventeen, Stimpson was still only five feet, six inches tall. But even if he hadn't grown much, physically, over the years, Stimpson had developed his God-given talent for elusiveness into a weapon that made him dangerous on the football field. So what if his helmet bobbled just a little as he ran?

Stimpson had been playing organized football since seventh grade—eighth grade, really. He had tried out for Jim Lowery's team in 1980, but as was often the case, the gruff coach's harsh attempts at motivation had the opposite effect. "He was very tough on me because I was little," Stimpson said. "I remember running through the suspended car tires. I got hung up in them one time and Coach Lowery said I needed bicycle tires to run through. That was it for me."

Before long, though, Stimpson was embarrassed at himself for walking off the practice field. So, with a little encouragement from the public address announcer, of all people, Stimpson decided to give football another shot. "I only lived a quarter of a mile from the school, as the crow flies," he said. After quitting, Stimpson occasionally stood outside his house during junior varsity homes games and listened as his friends' names echoed across Lookout Mountain. "You could hear the announcer just as if you were sitting in the bleachers," Stimpson said. "I played every year after that." When he returned to the team, Stimpson turned football into a productive outlet for his rambunctiousness. "I was not a punk on the football field; I did what they told me," he said. "So while I would destroy my character behind the scenes, if coaches told me to do something I tried to do it."

Still, Stimpson admitted that he was not beyond committing a prank or two at the expense of his teammates. "We had a water fountain outside the football field that was just a piece of PVC pipe with a bunch of holes drilled in it. During water breaks at practice I'd go up to it and blow in one of the holes and get everybody else soaking wet." Or Stimpson might sneak into the locker room a few minutes before practice and pour liquid heat into another player's jockstrap. "I can still hear Dan Andrews screaming from across the room when he put his jock on," Stimpson said. "I just tried to tick people off, mess with them."

Three people Stimpson never messed with were his coaches. He quickly came to realize that Jacoway, along with assistants James Rowe and Roland Hendon, genuinely cared about the boys on the team and wanted them to succeed in all aspects of their lives. "We did what the coaches said, period," he said. Stimpson remembered one day at practice when the offense was having a tough time getting the handle on a new wrinkle the coaching staff wanted to install for an upcoming opponent. After running the same play over and over and getting it wrong every time, Stimpson muttered under his breath that he was "about to get pissed off." When Jacoway responded by shouting back, for everyone to hear, that "some of you *need* to get pissed off," Stimpson was mortified, not because he kept making the same mistake but because he realized his coach had heard him swear. "I just wanted to crawl under a rock," he said.

Whatever the error at practice had been, Stimpson and his teammates must have figured it out, because by the end of the season Sand Rock's tiny tailback—all 135 pounds of him—had carried the majority of the load for the Wildcats, rushing 222 times for 1,225 yards. The highlight of it all, though, may have been Stimpson's game against Gaylesville in week five.

Thanks to wins over Cedar Bluff and Valley Head, all Sand Rock had to do in week five to claim the Area 16 championship was defeat the Trojans, another cross-country rival. Like the Wildcats, Gaylesville had already beaten area foes Valley Head and Spring Garden and was 3-1. The opposition unwittingly generated bulletin board material for the Wildcats a few days before the game with comments that appeared in the *Gadsden Times*. Regarding the previous year's game, a 27–23 loss at Sand Rock, Gaylesville's head coach admitted that he did not feel his team had lost. "Time just ran out on us," he said. In the same article, Jacoway told reporter Bill Lumpkin that his defense had been unable to control Gaylesville's wishbone attack in the '84 matchup and knew the Trojans "were upset and thought they should have won." Jacoway also knew that he and Rowe, his defensive coordinator, had come up with a seemingly foolproof plan for shutting down Valley Head's wishbone later that year in the playoffs. But he never tipped his hand to the reporter from the *Times*. "We know we're going to have to play a mistake-free game," Jacoway said. "They are going to be gunning for us."

Perhaps rapt by their own reporting, most of the sportswriters at the *Times* had the game figured for a nail-biter. Assistant sports editor John Allred predicted a 15–13 Sand Rock victory, and editor Jimmy Smothers even picked the Trojans to win. On Friday night, either Gaylesville played with their helmets on backward or Rowe's "mayday" defense was still an unsolved mystery to every other football coach in northeast Alabama. Whatever the reason, Sand Rock held the Trojans to 67 yards rushing and less than 100 yards of total offense. On the other side of the ball, Stimpson performed his Steve Austin impression up and down both sidelines. His 170 rushing on the ground included scoring runs of 64 and 34 yards. Gaylesville's only points of the game came on a blocked punt in the Wildcat end zone. The final score was 42–8. If anyone was biting their nails after that outcome, it was the five head coaches who still had Sand Rock on their schedules.

Today, Stimpson, like the rest of the adults among us, is no longer the juvenile he once was. A dedicated husband and father, he is as involved as possible in whatever is going on at Sand Rock High. "I feel like I owe the school, and I want to pay them back because even though I did all those things and most of the people there probably knew I was a rowdy punk, they loved me anyway," he said. "Coach Jacoway took a chance on me when a lot of coaches probably would not have, and I thank him for that and for teaching me all the lessons I have applied to my life—about having class, not giving up and treating every day as 'game day.'"

To this day, Stimpson believes that no other combination of people could have achieved what the Wildcats did in the fall of '85. "I am convinced that without the exact coaches we had, without every individual on the team just as they were, we would not have enjoyed the same success." Fortunately, the coaches and players meshed perfectly, and the successes kept piling up. Like many of his former teammates, Stimpson does not remember the final score from every game or even the exact order of the schedule. Like most of them, though, he does remember the sense of accomplishment that formed and grew within all of them as the weeks ticked by and the wins kept coming. "I remember playing 'Another One Bites the Dust,' 'We Are the Champions' and 'We Will Rock You,' in the field house after every game," Stimpson said. "I remember having so many people love us, lift us up and believe in us all the way to the end."

Stimpson and his teammates had already accomplished so much—five straight wins, along with the team's second area championship and third-ever playoff appearance—and the regular season was only half over.

CHAPTER 9

ROLLING RIGHT ALONG

Despite the big win over Gaylesville, which secured the Area 16 championship and a first-round home playoff game, the focus during Monday's team meeting and film session wasn't on how well the offense had executed the game plan or how dominant the defense had been—it was on Ricky Snider's backside. Snider, a junior, was a starting defensive lineman who had developed a boil "on a delicate area of his backside," Jamie Pitts remembered. Snider played in a three-point stance in front of linebacker Artie Mackey, whose job was to indicate the direction he would take on stunts and blitzes with a slap on the appropriate area of the nearest down lineman's rear end. "Ricky had told everybody not to hit him on his boil, but I guess Artie forgot," Pitts said. "He reached up, right before the snap, and whacked Ricky on that boil. Ricky shot straight up and went to yelling." Pitts figured the entire team was in for some extra laps come Monday because Snider swore all the way to the sideline. "But as he got closer he also got quieter, so Coach Jacoway wouldn't hear him." Jacoway had a little fun with the incident at Monday's practice, repeatedly rewinding the game film and replaying the hilarious scene. With the possible exception of Snider, the players' laughter roared louder every time.

Sand Rock's first two games in October were against private institutions. First up was Donoho, formerly known as Anniston Academy, followed by a road game against Madison Academy, near Huntsville. As usual, the defense had strong showings. Against the Falcons at home, the Wildcats won 14–3. The defense gave up only 166 yards, but a sloppy offensive performance drew Jacoway's ire in the post-game locker room. The following week, Jacoway's play packets featured a playful cover page with the words, "The Rock goes to the big city. Show off time!" Running back Jim Tom Stimpson remembered what Jacoway did to make light of any haughtiness his players might be subjected to because of their more pastoral home environment. "Coach mockingly gave their public address announcer a roster that included our full names, middle initial and everything," Stimpson said. "It was weird hearing our formal names called out after each play." So it was that James Thomas Stimpson Jr. scored the first touchdown against Madison Academy, and Thomas Wayne Steele added the point-after. The Wildcats, suddenly reinvigorated after their sluggish performance against Donoho, put on a rip-roaring good show and stretched the final score to 21–0 before heading home with a sense of entitlement of their own. They were 7-0, after all.

Senior standout Dwain "Bubba" Boyd had scored one of Sand Rock's two touchdowns against Donoho. The South Carolina transplant came to Lookout Mountain in 1983, just in time to join the football team as a sophomore and meet the team's new head coach. Unlike many of his teammates, however, Boyd had been playing organized football since second grade. By his senior year, he had acquired the size, speed and skill to be one of the best inside linebackers in north Alabama. At six feet, one inch and 190 pounds, Boyd wasn't very easy to bring down on the rare occasions when he lined up at fullback and barreled into the opposing defense, either.

Much like Jamie Pitts, Boyd had turned to football to fill a void in his life. He had followed his father, a building contractor, to Alabama only to have his dad return to South Carolina a short time later. Boyd's mother hardly ever came to see him play, and the lack of support at home for his football aspirations still stings today. "Daddy never saw me play as a junior or senior, and my mother only came to homecoming my senior year," Boyd said. "That's the only time she ever saw me play ball, and it was a huge disappointment to me. To be honest, I was a little bit ashamed of it." Late in the Wildcats' playoff run, when Jacoway chose Boyd, Stimpson and Lance Mackey to sit down for an interview with a local newspaper, the reporter asked Boyd about his parents. "I actually

Dwain "Bubba" Boyd had more game experience than just about anyone else on the team. The South Carolina transplant had begun playing football in second grade. *From the 1986 edition of the* Wildcat.

told a lie, that my daddy did come to all the games," he said. "I wanted to be like everybody else, which wasn't the case."

In lots of other ways, however, Boyd was very much like his teammates. He held down a part-time job, listened to the same music and motored around in a ramshackle, secondhand car. Actually, Boyd's ride might have been the most dilapidated vehicle in a parking lot filled with hand-me-downs, especially for a bruising inside linebacker. "I drove a little Volkswagen Beetle that was supposed to be red but had faded to pink," he said. Once, while he was trying to pass a school bus on a long, straight stretch of road, Boyd found out exactly how much car he did not have. "Jamie Pitts and I pulled out to pass and I followed alongside that bus for a half-mile until another car started coming," he said. "I actually had to stop and get back behind the bus because there was no go in that car."

There was plenty of go in Boyd, though. Usually on Saturday mornings, Boyd had to roll himself out of bed and doctor various cuts, bruises and scratches before heading to work. "One thing we always tried to do was leave everything we had on the field," Boyd said. "We were coached: Don't leave any regrets out there, do everything you had to do, sacrifice everything you have to sacrifice to get the job done." Over the course of the season, Boyd would eventually compile nearly five hundred yards rushing, and on the defensive side of the ball he was determined to break the team record for tackles in a season, a personal goal he soon realized he'd have been better off keeping to himself.

Somewhere about week eight, Boyd realized he was getting close to the magic number, which, as far as he could tell from studying the school's trophy case, had been established back in the 1970s. "I wanted to break that record," he said. "Ronnie Shaw had made 99 tackles, and I was at around 80 or so with about three games to go." One day in the weight room, Boyd was talking with Lance Mackey about the goal he had set for himself when Coach Jacoway walked in and overheard part of the conversation. "He ran up to me in a mad dash. I told him I was going for the record, and he said if he ever heard me talk about an individual record he'd kick me off the team," said Boyd. "I never mentioned it again." But Boyd did not forget his objective or let Jacoway's public admonishment prevent him from mangling any ball carrier who made the mistake of running in his general direction. Boyd figured the more tackles he made, the better off the team would be. By the end of the Repton game, he had slammed ball carriers to the ground 172 times—30 more tackles than anyone else on the team.

Boyd said that he still remembers the scolding Jacoway gave him about his personal aspirations as if it were yesterday and remains mindful of the message. "Whether Coach Jacoway knows it or not, and I've never told him, I leaned on him to fill the void I had because my daddy lived so far away." Boyd said he will never forget exactly where he was standing or the expression on Jacoway's face on the day he learned that individual aspirations should never come before the good of the team. "That moment had a lifelong impact on me," he said. "After that, I always felt like if you take care of the team then the other accolades will come."

Boyd might have thought he was in for a good cussing when he saw his head coach spring toward him in the locker room. Luckily, Jacoway hardly ever swore at anyone, and certainly not during his delivery of a life lesson, not even one disguised as a fit of rage in order to ensure maximum effect. On the other hand, after witnessing a few of another senior's on-the-field antics, even Reverend Billy Graham might have found himself cramming folding money into the swear jar.

Chapter 10

Alma Mater Doesn't Matter

As he watched film of the Collinsville game with his players after the Wildcats' win in week eight, Russell Jacoway had plenty of reasons to be pleased. The Wildcats had defeated his alma mater, 51–0, in front of a massive home crowd. It was a game Jacoway had desperately wanted to win, for many reasons. The Collinsville coach, despite helping Jacoway get his new job, had warned that there was little success to be had at Sand Rock because the talent level there was lacking. Also, the entire Lookout Mountain community was still smarting from a 68–0 whipping at the hands of their elevation-deprived neighbors back in 1982.

Lyndon Tidwell, a senior lineman on the '85 team, remembered Jacoway wanting to beat the Panthers in the worst way. "That was a big emotional rivalry for all of us," Tidwell said. "But Coach Jacoway wanted to destroy them." On Friday, the visiting team's pre-game attempt at intimidation had an unintended effect on tailback Jim Tom Stimpson. Gathered in an adjacent dressing room separated by a metal door, the Collinsville players began chanting and banging on the door just before they took the field. Stimpson couldn't believe what he was hearing, and he still remembers the thought that flashed through his mind. *Where are their coaches? They're going to have to pay for that!* "It was the most rude, undisciplined thing I had ever witnessed," Stimpson said. "That night ended up being the most lopsided beating we dished out the entire season."

Pretty much everyone got in on the action, too. Tommy Steele opened the scoring with a short field goal. The Panthers would have been wise to show more respect in the dressing room, because it was a still-fired-up Stimpson who set up Steele's kick with a seventy-one-yard run. Stimpson also scored the first touchdown of the game on a fifty-yard scamper a few minutes later. Lance Mackey completed six of eight pass attempts, including touchdown tosses to Artie Mackey, Jeff Whaley and Dewayne Heard. Along the way, Whaley scored on a two-point conversion pass and snagged an interception that set up another trip into the end zone. Steele, who usually compiled his points one at a time, got six on a two-yard run late in the game to close out the scoring.

Three days later, Jacoway was sitting in the dark with his coaches and players, watching the pounding he had been so eager to administer to the school at which he had been part of a state title–winning basketball team in 1975. He might have even been trying to think up an appropriate way to officially observe the Wildcats' big win—maybe even celebrate, somehow. Suddenly, out of the corner of his eye, he caught a glimpse of…something…that wiped the smile right off his face.

"What the hell was that?!" The question came abruptly and loudly, surpising everyone in the darkened room. For starters, the players rarely heard Jacoway swear. Assistants James Rowe and Roland Hendon had just assumed that their boss was aware of the clowning around that one of the starting cornerbacks—a senior no less—had been guilty of for the past several games. Everyone else in the stadium certainly was. Several times, Jacoway stopped the video cassette player, rewound the tape and hit play. Finally, the poor-quality image came into focus well enough for Jacoway to make out a jersey number. This produced another shout. "Was that you, Heard?!"

Jamie Pitts assumed that everyone already knew about the latest eighties fad to hit Sand Rock High School: Dewayne Heard's backfield boogie. "Sometimes late in the game, when we were ahead a little bit, Dewayne was bad to get out there and do this break dance stuff," Pitts said. "He'd get out there and spin on his helmet. It had been happening for several games." With the visiting Collinsville Panthers completely caged late in the going, Heard had busted yet another of his patented moves between plays by bending over, kicking his legs into the air and spinning on his helmet. This time, the camera operator had panned away from the line of scrimmage just long enough for Heard's head spin to make the highlight reel. "I don't know how Coach Jacoway never noticed it before," Pitts said, with no hint of a grin. "I guess he was busy watching the football game." When he did finally notice, Jacoway was fit to be tied, and punishment was administered across the board. "Coach asked him when he started doing that, and Dewayne told him he'd been doing it for three or four games," Pitts said. "I told him to shut up or we'd be running all night."

Tight end Dewayne Heard was a character off the field and sometimes on it. But teammates agreed that he was "all business" once the ball was snapped. *From the 1986 edition of the* Wildcat.

Heard was another transplant from outside Cherokee County and had been playing football since moving to Sand Rock in 1982. If there was another prankster on the team besides Stimpson, it was the wiry, feather-haired receiver who had moved to Lookout Mountain from Pisgah. Once, during a game played in a driving rain at Sand Rock, Heard noticed the other team's offensive linemen had become hesitant to place their hands on the field when they got into their three-point stances because the ground was wiggling with earthworms driven to the surface by the standing water. "Dewayne was always a little…off, I guess," Jeff Whaley said. "He looked over at me and winked."

Heard grabbed an earthworm, stuck it in his mouth, turned to the opposing linemen and grinned wide. "There was an end of that worm sticking out each side of his mouth," Whaley said. "They didn't want to get close to Dewayne for the rest of the night." Lyndon Tidwell had a similar recollection of Heard's on-the-field demeanor. "He had a crazy attitude," Tidwell said. "He'd run over and head butt the goal post at practice."

Heard might have been prone to a little good-natured goofing off between plays, but he was all business at the snap. Like a lot of the players on the '85 team, Heard played both ways. On offense he was one of Lance Mackey's go-to receivers and contributed seventy-three tackles and six interceptions on defense. "He gave 110 percent all the time," Tidwell said. In fact, Heard played the last half of the season with a pinched nerve in his shoulder, never once complaining. He needed regular treatment for the injury but had no car. For several consecutive weeks in the last half of the season, Pitts, himself nursing a knee injury, drove Heard to a local chiropractor. "Mr. Pearson, the principal, would check us both out of school," Pitts said. "I would drop Dewayne off in Centre, and then I'd drive to a doctor in Rome to get my knee worked on. I'd pick Dewayne up on my way back, and we'd go to football practice." Pitts said it was months before anyone knew about the two of them leaving school on an almost daily basis to keep themselves physically prepared to play. "That went on for a long time," Pitts said. "I'm sure my dad still doesn't know about that."

The chiropractic treatments must have been effective. In a 26–9 win over Westminster in week nine, Lance Mackey threw four touchdowns and Heard caught two of them. The win brought good news on several fronts: Mackey was nearing one thousand passing yards for the year (he would finish the season with over fourteen hundred yards through the air, plus another five hundred on the ground), and the Wildcats' number two ranking in Class 1A was further solidified. Also, the school was only one win away from its first undefeated regular season in history. With the exception of one well-educated man who had been watching Sand Rock football seasons go down the drain for decades, most Wildcats fans considered the latest developments to be extremely encouraging. The majority of the maroon-and-white contingent on Lookout Mountain eagerly anticipated the chance to line up against an opponent in week ten that promised to provide some quality competition. Principal L.D. Pearson, on the other hand, was just about ready to call the whole thing off.

Chapter 11

The Longest Time

If anyone had the right to pine for Sand Rock's perfection on the football field, it was L.D. Pearson. He had been the principal at the school since before the program's revival in 1965 and had endured unending humiliation, season after season, for almost every one of those twenty years. Pearson loved his school and the game of football and had grown to hate the Wildcats' unshakeable knack for losing. He simply wanted to see his Wildcats succeed, even if he felt he needed to intervene on the rare occasion when someone made what he considered a scheduling snafu.

When Pearson realized that there was a chance that the school's first-ever undefeated season could end prematurely at the hands of a larger, faster, more powerful team from West End–Walnut Grove, Pearson was willing to pull the plug on the Wildcats' game in week ten. Nine wins and no losses was good enough for Pearson, and he made no apologies for the way he felt. "I told him we would have to play, because if we cancelled the game it would be considered a forfeit and we'd lose, anyway," Russell Jacoway said.

Pearson was right to be concerned about the outcome against the Patriots, at least on paper. West End was ranked number two in the state in Class 2A and had lost only once all season. In fact, the Patriots had beaten four schools from bigger, faster, stronger Class 3A, including the Susan Moore Bulldogs, a team that eventually made it into the

L.D. Pearson had been principal at Sand Rock since before the Wildcats football team returned to the field in 1965. In 1986, the senior class honored Pearson's longtime commitment to the school by dedicating the yearbook to him. *From the 1986 edition of the* Wildcat.

quarterfinal round of the playoffs. In an article two days before the game, *Gadsden Times* sportswriter Bill Lumpkin predicted that the Sand Rock versus West End game would feature "two of the toughest defenses in the state." But in the same article, Patriots coach Wayne Robinson made it clear that he disagreed with such a simplistic evaluation. "We play in different classes, so I think it would be hard to compare the defenses," he told Lumpkin. He went on to mention that Sand Rock was "a well-coached team and they don't make many mistakes." One mistake Russell Jacoway did not want his players to make was looking ahead to the first round of the playoffs, and he said as much to Lumpkin. "We won't have any motivational problem for this game," Jacoway said. "Sand Rock has never had an undefeated season and that will be motivation enough."

On Thursday, sportswriters at the *Times* made it clear they did not think the possibility of going 10-0 would be sufficient incentive for Sand

Rock. Only one of the "Gridiron Guessperts" predicted Sand Rock to defeat West End. Assistant Sports Editor John Alred, while admitting that defense would likely decide the game, obviously did not like Sand Rock's chances; he picked the Patriots by the score of 12–8. The slight did not overly offend the Wildcats, though, because over the years they had become accustomed to playing in games they were expected to lose. "Coach always said we played several homecoming games a year," Lance Mackey joked. "When I was a sophomore, we played one at home and probably five on the road." Jacoway made light of the situation on the cover page of his play sheet handout that week: "You are expected to be nice and mind your manners because you were scheduled as the SOFT touch on West End's schedule," it read.

Jacoway probably didn't appreciate having his team measured for their caskets by a bunch of knuckleheaded newspapermen before the first whistle even sounded, but he did recognize their concerns. During practice that week, Jacoway warned his players to be prepared for a more physically demanding opponent than they had seen all season. "They are very big and physical, and our defense must be more physical than they have been all year," he told his team. "The key to winning this game," he said, "is hit, hit, hit, hit, hit!"

Come Friday, there were collisions aplenty. As usual, Lance Mackey led the way for Sand Rock with an early 17-yard touchdown pass to Jeff Whaley. As predicted, though, it was the defense that shined. Assisted by horrible field conditions caused by heavy rains, the Patriots held the Wildcats to a paltry 54 yards rushing and only 4 yards over the final two quarters. The Sand Rock defense was also able to find traction in the slick mud. Lance Mackey led the way from his spot at cornerback, intercepting two passes and recovered a fumble. The rest of the Wildcats did their part, as well, pounding the West End running backs all night and giving up only 136 total yards. Years later, assistant coach Roland Hendon remembered how well the defense played that night, but he also recalled another factor that he believes helped determine the final outcome. "One of their running backs had been hurt the week before, and that happened to us two or three times during the year," he said. "We were a good football team, but sometimes you have to be a little lucky to go undefeated."

Lucky or not, the Wildcats held the Patriots out of the end zone, and junior tailback Scott Norris added a late touchdown to extend the final score to 14–0. Sand Rock completed its first-ever undefeated regular season against, ironically, the first opponent its football team had ever beaten. (Walnut Grove, which Sand Rock had defeated, 7–6, in 1945, had combined with Altoona in 1966 to form West End High School; many from the older generation still refer to the institution by its combined name, West End–Walnut Grove.) As Mackey, Norris, Whaley and their teammates made their way back to the locker room to change out of their filthy uniforms and load up for the bus ride home, they whooped and hollered, ecstatic to be a part of the school's first-ever undefeated season.

But they were not satisfied. Not yet. The other goal, which they only mentioned to one another after summer practices or in the hallways between classes, suddenly seemed not only attainable but also almost destined to become reality. All the Wildcats had to do now was want that championship trophy badly enough to go out and get it. "At the beginning of the season I don't think anybody in their wildest dreams thought we'd go that far," Jeff Whaley said. "But once we got into the playoffs after beating West End, which was a bigger school that no one had given us a chance against, I think it really started clicking in our minds that we had a chance to win it all." The playoffs, on the horizon since halfway through the season, had finally arrived. The Wildcats had whipped the local competition; now was the time to see how well they matched up against the rest of Alabama. First up was a home game on November 8 against Speake.

Chapter 12

FOR THOSE ABOUT TO ROCK

The Wildcats had finished the regular season without a loss and were locked in at number two in the Class 1A poll. But despite those heady numbers, several members of the team remained upset at what they perceived to be a consistent lack of respect from the Gadsden media. Often, stories recounting the Wildcats' wins were relegated to page two or three in the Saturday sports section. Also, the paper almost never sent a photographer to Sand Rock games, and in the week leading up to the week-ten contest against West End almost none of the sportswriters had given Sand Rock a fighting chance. So, the day after they and their teammates pounded the Patriots, seniors Jamie Pitts, Jim Tom Stimpson and Dewayne Heard decided that someone ought to send a message to those know-nothings. "We borrowed Jim Tom's granddaddy's old orange truck," Pitts said. "And we got eight of the biggest rocks we could find from his farm, and we got some paint."

The trio slathered six of the huge boulders with the final scores from all ten games and then emblazoned two others with the words "We Want Respect." "They were big boulders that had come off the farm," Pitts said. "One was as big as a dining room table." After loading the rocks into the back of the old International, the three returned to their homes for supper. Later than night, after everyone else had gone to bed, Pitts and Stimpson snuck out of their homes, climbed into W.C. "Dub" Stimpson's old pickup and set out for the Times building in downtown

Gadsden. "Jim Tom was so little he looked like a child driving that truck, and we had so much weight in the bed that the front wheels were barely touching the ground," Pitts said. "It's a wonder we didn't get killed. Or caught—that would have been much worse."

Somehow, about midnight, Pitts and Stimpson made it to Gadsden and slowed to a stop in front of the main entrance of the Times. "We pulled up to the building and saw somebody in there working," Pitts said. "We just started unloading rocks." Pitts and Stimpson positioned seven of the rocks in front of the Times, completely blocking the main entrance. Another boulder ended up at the back door of a local radio station that awarded a "Team of the Week" trophy every Friday morning. (Despite being 10-0, the Wildcats had never graced the airwaves.) "At the end of season, after they named us their Team of the Year, they covered that rock with Q-104 decals and gave it back to us," Pitts said.

The following week, Assistant Sports Editor John Alred responded to the late-night landscaping job. "Evidently, some Sand Rock fans feel their team is the Rodney Dangerfield of high school football. They get no respect." Alred admitted that the previous week's "presents" were probably a result of his sportswriters siding with West End but stopped short of an apology. "I have plenty of respect for Sand Rock," Alred wrote. "Any team, regardless of class, that has an 11-0 record certainly deserves respect." At that point in the article, though, Alred could not resist a dig at his detractors. He explained that a *Times* employee moved the rocks, which weighed "about 150 pounds each," to his home and built a walkway from his house to a utility room. "They were just the thing he needed for his backyard," Alred jabbed. He also wrote that he called Russell Jacoway to try to get to the bottom of the "prank," as he called it. "I don't mind a little kidding, as long as they don't decide to deposit the rocks on my car."

Pitts and Stimpson kept the story of their midnight adventure to themselves as long as they could stand it…which was not very long. "At school on Monday we told everybody it was us who had done it," Pitts said. If Jacoway found out that three of his players were responsible for a half-ton of rocks rolling their way down Highway 411 in the middle of the night, he did not let on. "We never got in trouble with Coach Jacoway for that," Pitts said. "He just snickered and never mentioned

Jim Tom Stimpson (wearing sunglasses) and Jamie Pitts hoist the rock they left at a Gadsden radio station the night after the West End game. When the Wildcats were named the Q-104 Team of the Year, the station covered the rock with decals and presented it to the team. *From the scrapbook of Dan Andrews.*

it again." Pitts said he still recounts the tale of that night from time to time and never fails to tickle himself. "I can still picture Jim Tom holding onto that steering wheel," Pitts laughed. "He was not looking over the wheel, he was so small that he had to look through the spokes to see out to drive."

Believe it or not, in the United States of America as it existed twenty-five years ago, the lack of modern technology allowed for more freedom, especially for any kid with a driver's license. In 1985, text messaging cellphones and GPS tracking systems were still decades away from finding their way into everyone's hip pockets, so it was actually possible for a couple of teenagers to take off to a town thirty miles away and stay gone for a couple of hours without anyone getting wise—or even taking the time to worry about where they might be. There was no quick way to find out someone's location back then, so questions regarding the previous night's whereabouts either got asked later or sometimes not at all. "I reckon we pulled it off without our daddies finding out, because surely they'd have both beat the hell out of us if they'd known," Pitts said.

Sand Rock's first-round playoff game, over Area 15 runner-up Speake, went about as most people expected, though during the week Coach Jacoway made sure to remind his players not to take the Bobcats for granted. "We'd better get excited about this game," Jacoway told the *Times*. "If we don't it could be a sad night for us." Speake had only won once, Jacoway noted, but "five of their losses were by less than six points, so their record could easily be better."

Speake's record did not improve after the trip to Sand Rock. Lance Mackey hit Artie Mackey for a fifty-one-yard touchdown early in the game for a 7–0 lead. After the defense stopped the Bobcats on three consecutive plays, Mackey pitched to tailback Jim Tom Stimpson on an apparent sweep at the thirty-two-yard line. For the first time all season, instead of darting toward the sideline, the shifty tailback pulled up and lobbed the ball over several defenders, right into the arms of a streaking Dewayne Heard. Touchdown. Lance Mackey added two more scoring passes, another to Heard just before halftime and a twenty-five-yard strike to Jeff Whaley in the fourth quarter. Mackey also scored from forty-four yards out after calling for a quick snap from center Clayton Robertson. Speake's inside linebackers had left the middle of the field unoccupied when they suspected another toss sweep and shifted over to try and stop Stimpson. Mackey blasted down the middle of the field untouched. The final score was 34–0, setting up a rematch in round two with cross-county rival Cedar Bluff, which had won its opening round game at Appalachian.

Chapter 13

ONE THING LEADS TO ANOTHER

Sand Rock's road game in the second round of the playoffs did not require a long trip. Cedar Bluff is only about twenty minutes away, on the other side of Weiss Lake. The small shoreline town was home to the team that had come closer than any other to outlasting the Wildcats during the regular season. Tiger fans felt that their team had whipped the Wildcats back in week two and did not mind saying so. When Cedar Bluff's student correspondent to the *Cherokee County Herald* submitted a column recapping the Tigers' win in the opening round of the playoffs at Appalachian, he could not help including a few mocking remarks that quickly made their way onto the bulletin board in the Sand Rock locker room:

> *Next on the hit list is a team we beat everywhere but the scoreboard the last time we bumped heads. This time the scoreboard is going to be in on the deal. This game is going to be one that will never be forgotten.*

The Tigers had limped their way through the regular season with a record of 5-5, mostly by winning at home and losing on the road. With the exception of the loss to Sand Rock, Cedar Bluff had won all the games that mattered and finished as the runners-up in Area 16. Thanks to their 35–7 thumping of the Eagles the previous week, the Tigers had earned the right to a rematch with Sand Rock.

Russell Jacoway told *Gadsden Times* assistant sports editor John Alred that he expected another defensive struggle. "Cedar Bluff is much better than the first time we played them," Jacoway said. "They certainly know how to play defense. In fact, they are the best defensive team we have played all year." In an attempt to motivate his offensive line, Jacoway heaped praise on the Tigers' defensive front. "The thing we've got to do this time…that we didn't do the first time is block," he said. "Our line just didn't do a good job. It looked like our backs were running into a brick wall. They just overpowered us." Actually, it was not the offensive line that had almost cost the Wildcats. The holes were there, and the running backs had picked up over two hundred yards darting through them. Unfortunately, they had also kept the game frighteningly close by fumbling the ball on two occasions.

Among the details Jacoway did not share with Alred was that he had been upset with himself over his play selection in the first game against Cedar Bluff. Perhaps because of some lingering uncertainty over Lance Mackey's passing abilities, Jacoway had mostly stuck to the ground game. Called upon only in the most obvious situations, Mackey had finished the game a horrible one-of-nine passing for only fifteen yards and two interceptions. The one-dimensional attack had kept the game closer than it should have been, Jacoway thought. If it had not been for the defense's ability to force two crucial Cedar Bluff turnovers, both during drives deep into Wildcat territory, the final score could easily have been the other way around or worse. Jacoway knew that if he wanted to avoid another close call at Bruce Field—one that might immediately cause everyone on Lookout Mountain to forget about an entire season's worth of incredible accomplishments—he was going to have to turn Lance Mackey loose.

Cedar Bluff's head coach had seen the same game film and knew exactly what was coming. "He [Mackey] is definitely the key for Sand Rock," Danny Brown told Alred for the same article. "There have been some teams able to stop their running game, but they haven't been able to stop Mackey." Over the first eleven weeks of the '85 season, Brown's star running back, senior tailback David Blevins, had amassed over 1,500 yards rushing and twenty-three touchdowns, but Mackey had already equaled that output with his combined running and passing. Plus, Brown was convinced that Mackey had become a lot more comfortable with the offense over the past couple of months. "The first time we played this season both teams had opportunities to score, but each time the other team's defense stopped it," Brown said. "Since then, Sand Rock's passing attack has improved considerably."

Cherokee County High School is just down the road from Cedar Bluff. In the fall of 1985, excitement had been high in nearby Centre because the football team was the defending Class 4A runners-up. Then, the Warriors lost their opening-round playoff game against Alexandria, leaving thousands of football-starved fans in Cherokee County with nothing better to do on the second Friday in November than drive five miles to watch Cedar Bluff battle Sand Rock. The contest was, quite literally, the only game in town. Earlier in the week, temporary bleachers had been trucked in from nearby baseball fields to handle the anticipated crowd, and by Friday afternoon several oversized grills had been set up behind the concession stand and were overloaded with extra hot dogs and beef patties. Hopefully, the homemade cheeseburgers were worth the cost of admission, because the game was a blowout:

> *The second time around proved a little easier for Sand Rock. And it might have been a little sweeter.*

So began sportswriter Henry Reynolds' recount in the November 16, 1985 edition of the *Gadsden Times*. The final score was 21–7, but the game never seemed that close. Sand Rock opened the scoring midway through the first quarter after beginning at its own thirty-three. Jim Tom Stimpson covered the final twenty-nine yards in dramatic fashion, shucking and slipping his way to the sideline and then outrunning a host of defenders to the end zone. Tommy Steele's kick made the score 7–0. After a Cedar Bluff fumble, Jacoway released the reigns on his passing game, and Lance Mackey quickly fired a forty-seven-yard completion to Jeff Whaley, down to the eleven-yard line. Two plays later, Mackey passed to Dwain "Bubba" Boyd for a touchdown and a fourteen-point halftime lead.

Cedar Bluff finally got on the board in the third quarter after David Blevins returned the second-half kickoff to the Sand Rock forty-one. Ten plays later, Blevins dove in from the one, and senior Roy Mitchell kicked the extra point, pulling the Tigers to within seven. After both defenses spent the rest of the third quarter and half the fourth forcing punts, Sand Rock's offense found the end zone again and put the game out of reach. Mackey led a drive that took only six plays to cover forty-seven yards. He crossed the goal line himself from five yards out with just over six minutes remaining.

Cedar Bluff had nothing even remotely equivalent to Sand Rock's effective passing attack, so in the final minutes Brown was forced to move Blevins to quarterback and hope for another miraculous Hail Mary. As they had done in week two, the Tigers tried a gadget play late in the game. Lightning almost struck twice, but the stacked odds ended up working against Cedar Bluff when a long pass down to the six-yard line was nullified by a holding call. After the Tigers turned the ball over on downs, Sand Rock ran out the clock and upped its record to 12-0.

When Sand Rock and Cedar Bluff met early in the season, the Wildcats had committed four turnovers. In the playoff rematch, they never lost the ball. Cedar Bluff fumbled only once in its final game of the season, but the turnover was a costly one, leading to Mackey's long pass to Whaley and eventually a touchdown that put the game out of reach for the run-heavy Tigers. Danny Brown had practically predicted the result in his interview with the *Times* earlier in the week. "The outcome will probably be determined by the team that gets the big break early," he told Alred. Unfortunately for Cedar Bluff, Sand Rock got the first lucky bounce and never looked back. The following Monday afternoon, while the Tigers were in their dressing room cleaning out their lockers and turning in their equipment, the Wildcats were strapping theirs on, getting ready for the school's first-ever trip to the state quarterfinals.

CHAPTER 14

GLORY DAYS

After dominating the game at Cedar Bluff in round two, the Wildcats returned home to play in the quarterfinals. The "speedy Jackets," as *Gadsden Times* sportswriter Greg Bailey referred to Mount Hope in his weekly column, were also undefeated, ranked number three in the Class 1A poll. Coach Russell Jacoway told Bailey that the Yellow Jackets did indeed look fast on film. "It's hard for us to simulate that in practice," Jacoway said. "We're spending more time than usual on defense this week. They have three kids with more speed than anyone we've got."

Mount Hope's quarterback, Sammy Gholston, was among the speedsters Jacoway was talking about. The senior had been selected to the All-State First Team the year before and was so entrusted by his head coach that he was allowed to call his own plays. "Everyone I've talked to says he's the best athlete on the team," Jacoway told Bailey. Sand Rock linebacker Dwain "Bubba" Boyd had heard the same scuttlebutt. Earlier in the week, while he and Lance Mackey were talking in the Wildcats' locker room, Boyd made clear his intentions to put a stop to Gholston's impressive on-the-field antics. "I told Lance I was going to do everything I could to punish their quarterback so that Lance could get the same glory the other guy had gotten the year before," Boyd said.

On Friday November 22, as Bruce Springsteen's "Born in the U.S.A." blared over their stadium's tinny loudspeaker, the Wildcats busted through a banner that the Sand Rock cheerleaders had decorated with the likeness of a giant can of Raid. As soon as the game began, Boyd and the rest of the Wildcat defense swarmed the Yellow Jackets. After Lance Mackey and the offense took the opening kickoff and drove the length of the field for a touchdown, the three-deep crowd along the Wildcat sideline watched as Mount Hope's wishbone offense went three and out on its first series. The next time a Yellow Jacket touched the ball, he fumbled it right back to the Wildcats. After Sand Rock missed a short field goal attempt, Mount Hope went three and out again. And again.

The crowd began to howl "De-fense! De-fense!" After the Wildcats gave up a long pass play down to their own thirty-four-yard line, Boyd busted into the backfield on consecutive plays to kill another drive. Following a Sand Rock punt, Gholston tried a long pass, but Jeff Whaley stepped in front of the receiver, grabbed the ball and returned the interception to the eight-yard line. Still two yards from the end zone on third and goal, Jacoway decided that the best guy to send into his own offensive backfield was the player who had seemingly spent most of the night in Mount Hope's huddle. As Bubba Boyd bounded into the end zone to run the halftime score to 14–0, the home crowd changed its cheer to "Roll Rock Roll!"

In the second half, Boyd continued to spend significant time near the ball, supplying a key run up the middle for twenty yards in the third quarter and a big sack late in the game after Mount Hope's offense began passing on almost every down. The presumably "speedy" Yellow Jackets could not outrun anyone wearing a Sand Rock jersey and finished the night with only fifty-nine rushing yards. The final score was 17–0.

On the sideline, Boyd hustled back to the field house. Along the way he accepted congratulations from his teammates and coaches and felt satisfied that he had followed through on his promise to Mackey to shutdown the Jackets' hotshot QB. So was Coach Jacoway. "Dwain was with Mount Hope's quarterback all night," Jacoway told reporters. "They had a close relationship by the time the game was over." As they made their way toward the exits, the Wildcat faithful began chanting another challenge to Boyd and his teammates: "Two to Go! Two to Go!"

The following Friday in the quarterfinals, Sand Rock's opponent was a team from Carrollton that had been underestimated so far in the postseason, probably because of their 3-6 regular season record. But the

Junior running back Craig Twilley (35) stands alongside Head Coach Russell Jacoway, ready to enter the game against Carrollton. The Wildcats whipped the Indians 17–0 to advance to the state championship. *From the scrapbook of Dan Andrews.*

Indians had reeled off three straight playoff wins, and Russell Jacoway wanted to make certain his players did not start packing their bags for a trip to the championship game until the final whistle had blown. "I think they're the best team we've played this year," Jacoway said of the Indians. "The key for us is to get excited. If we do, we'll have a shot. If we don't we'll lose. That's exactly what I told the kids."

The kids must have gotten excited because the offense rolled up almost 250 yards of offense. Lance Mackey threw touchdown passes to Dewayne Heard and Jeff Whaley, and Tommy Steele added a field goal for another 17–0 victory. Carrollton's multiple-attack offense, which had racked up sixty-three points in its first three playoff games, managed only 63 yards against the Wildcats. Possibly the only Carrollton player that Sand Rock public address announcer Terry Teat knew from memory by the end of the night was the Indians' punter, who had run on and off the field nine times.

The next morning, as is customary during the state playoffs, coaches from all advancing teams attended a mandatory meeting at the Alabama High School Athletics Association headquarters in Montgomery. For Jacoway, Rowe and Hendon, the trip was about three hours each way; after the win over Carrollton, the trio was making its fourth consecutive Saturday morning drive. Not that they were complaining too loudly, since the only way to avoid the hassle was by losing. "'There will only be half as many of you here next week'—that was what AHSAA director Bubba Scott would tell us every week when he began the meeting," Hendon remembered. Still, all three coaches were reaching the point of complete exhaustion. "We got so tired of that trip," Hendon said. "We talked a lot of football on those rides, but for the last two weeks we mostly slept." At least once, everybody in the car was asleep at the same time. "I don't remember which game it was after, but we were all three just dog-tired on the way to Montgomery," Hendon said. "At one point, we woke up and we were in the grass median on the interstate—and still moving pretty fast!"

Hendon survived that trip to and from the state capital without a scratch. But on the way back from Montgomery the Saturday after the Carrollton game, Hendon was involved in an incident in downtown Birmingham that scarred half the people in the state of Alabama for life. "We were coming back, and Alabama and Auburn were playing at Legion Field," Hendon said. "We had two tickets between the three of us." Jacoway and Rowe, both Auburn graduates, took pity on Hendon and pooled their money with his so they could purchase a third ticket. After they entered the gate, Hendon shuffled off to find a seat among the forty-five thousand Crimson Tide fans, while Rowe and Jacoway joined the other half wearing orange and blue. (Until 1989, Legion Field served as a neutral site for the Iron Bowl. Ticket allotments were split down the middle, and the two universities took turns "hosting" the game.)

With under a minute remaining and the Tide down 23–22 on their own twelve-yard line, a disgusted Hendon began making his way toward the nearest exit. "I had gotten as far as the end zone when Van Tiffin ran onto the field." Hendon had missed one of the most amazing hurry-up drives in college football history but managed to elbow his way to a spot along the end zone fence just in time to see the Crimson Tide placekicker's dramatic, game-winning fifty-two-yard field goal come

Roland Hendon got the silent treatment from Auburn alums Russell Jacoway and James Rowe after Van Tiffin booted the game-winning field goal for the Crimson Tide in the final seconds of the 1985 Iron Bowl. The Kick, *painting by Daniel A. Moore © 2009 New Life Art, Inc. Used with permission.*

sailing directly toward him. Then, pandemonium. "I've never seen a place go wild like that," Hendon said. "People were running onto the field, not really towards anyone, just running every which way." Based on what he had seen for over fifty-nine minutes, Hendon had already prepared himself for an uncomfortable ride home. He still got one but happily spent those two hours trying to hide a grin. "They made me drive back and never said a word to me all the way," Hendon said. "That is a memory that I've probably enhanced over the years, but I love telling that story."

If Jacoway and Rowe still held a grudge toward Hendon after the Crimson Tide won the Iron Bowl, they did not let it affect their preparation for the state championship. Film of Repton's most recent games was watched repeatedly and dissected thoroughly; a game plan for attacking the Bulldogs was devised and distributed to the players in Jacoway's fifteenth and final backward-stapled packet. All three coaches had classes to teach, but substitutes had to be called in during the week because the phones would not stop ringing. Reporters wanted quotes and charter buses had to be scheduled, and there were hundreds of other smaller details that needed a coach's signature or nod of approval. The hallways were a madhouse. At least once during the week, no one could find Jacoway to take a reporter's phone call, so Hendon played the part. "I don't think anyone ever figured out the difference," Jacoway said. "He knew the answers to all the questions anyone might ask, anyway."

Another phone call Hendon was involved in that week was particularly interesting and served as a motivational tool for the coaching staff as they prepared for Repton. "I'll never forget, their principal called us up," Hendon said, "and since I was the assistant principal as well as a coach, Mr. Pearson called me into his office to hear the call." Repton principal David Johnson proceeded to instruct Pearson and Hendon on the correct procedures for conducting a brief post-game ceremony during which the second-place trophy would be presented. "He was implying that we would be the ones getting it, and he was instructing us what to do to receive

Lance Mackey (12), Artie Mackey, Jim Tom Stimpson (34) and Dwain Boyd (40) hoist the Class 1A state championship trophy during a ceremony in the Sand Rock gymnasium on December 11, 1985. *From the scrapbook of Dan Andrews.*

it," Hendon said. Immediately after the call ended Hendon sprinted to Jacoway's office to relate the story. By the end of the day, every player on the team knew about the Wildcats' latest dose of disrespect. "And you know, I don't remember them handing out the second-place trophy after that game," Hendon said with a smile.

A newspaper in Anniston, about fifty miles south of Sand Rock, finally took notice of the Wildcats' accomplishments a few days before the Repton game. Reporter Basil Penny eased his car through to the four-way stop, parked in front of an old country store and pulled up a rocking chair beside Jim Tom Stimpson's grandfather. The Tuesday morning air had brought "hog-killing weather" to Lookout Mountain, Penny wrote, but the only topic on the minds of the elderly gentlemen who spent their idle hours at Wells Grocery was Wildcat football. "I talked with a man down there at the Auburn-Alabama game," said "Dub" Stimpson. "He said Repton is little, but fast. So are we." Proprietor Alvis Wells said he was not figuring on breaking any sales records on Friday. "Everybody in the community will be in Repton, except for three firemen," Wells said with a laugh.

The morning after the game, the headline of *Gadsden Times* reporter Henry Reynolds's story from Repton read "Sand Rock Wins Class A Crown." In his first sentence, Reynolds reminded his readers of a preseason prediction that had never received much attention from the press:

> *Sand Rock's dream of winning the state Class 1A high school football championship became a reality here Friday night as the Wildcats defeated Repton 14–6. James Rowe, assistant coach for Sand Rock, predicted in August, before a single game was played, "If anyone beats us it'll be an upset." His words held true.*

In the days ahead, Reynolds reported in-depth on the Sand Rock football team's complete transition from second-best to first-rate: In fifteen games, the offense had scored 400 points and the defense had allowed only 53. During the playoffs, the Wildcats outscored their five opponents 103–13. The list of individual accolades for players and coaches would not be made official for several weeks, but when postseason awards were finally announced, newspapers were filled with

Sand Rock athletes, most notably members of the championship-winning football team, enjoyed a table filled with awards at the school's annual sports banquet in the spring of 1986. *From the scrapbook of Jim Tom Stimpson.*

the names of Sand Rock players, including at least one who did not realize the significance of the compliment.

Lance Mackey was among the first Wildcats to find out he had been voted All-State First Team, and Dwain "Bubba" Boyd was a little surprised when Mackey called to relay the news because he did not know any such thing existed. "I had no idea what All-State even was," Boyd admitted. "To me it sounded like the most unachievable thing in the world." But Boyd had earned the honors, as had fellow seniors Lance Mackey, Mark Parker and Jeff Whaley. Junior Ricky Snider was also voted to the team, and senior lineman Chris St. Clair received an honorable mention. The *Birmingham News* voted Mackey and Boyd to their All-State team. Heard, Stimpson, Pitts, Artie Mackey, Tommy Steele and Dewayne Heard, along with Lance Mackey and Boyd, were also named to the Area 16 All-Area team. Junior lineman Dan Andrews joined several of his teammates on the All-County team.

Alabama sportswriters did not overlook the impressive turnaround Russell Jacoway had performed, either. Both the *Birmingham News* and *Associated Press* named him the Class 1A Coach of the Year. With a state title under his belt so early in his career, the youthful Collinsville native could have probably gone just about anywhere, demanded a higher salary and eventually worked his way up to a head coach's job at a big school like Hoover or Prattville—maybe even a position on a college staff. The old-timers who spent their spare time sitting around the potbellied stove at Wells Grocery must also have been wondering just how much longer they would be lucky enough to keep their new coach. Based on how frequently the football job at Sand Rock typically became vacant, the athletic boosters might have seriously considered the appointment of a permanent search team. But if they ever got around to selecting a committee chairman, he is still waiting to gavel his first meeting to order.

Chapter 15

FIRE ON THE MOUNTAIN

At a glance, the football field and surrounding area still appear much the same today as a quarter-century ago, though there have been a few upgrades over the years. Aluminum bleachers now line the Wildcat sidelines and are a significant improvement over the cinder blocks and two-by-fours first erected in the mid-1960s. Just behind the home seating sits a field house that did not exist in 1985. Built in the early 1990s, the corrugated metal building features a film room complete with theatre seating, an expanded weight room and a hand-laid rock wall in the varsity locker room. Another round of expansion, already underway in the fall of 2009, will further modernize the computer technology in the film room and add additional office and storage space. Team uniforms have also been enhanced over the years. Updated jerseys and pants now feature a splash of black here and there, and the brush script "Wildcats" on the helmets has given way to a more contemporary representation of the school mascot.

A look around from midfield reveals a few modifications on the landscape. In the end zones, the old H-shaped goal posts have given way to a modern "Y" design; the ramshackle press box still straddles the fifty-yard line, although today it is one story taller than a generation ago thanks to recycled slats of lumber taken off the original home-side grandstands. Across the street, the town of Sand Rock—incorporated in 1988—has built a pair of athletic fields and a public playground alongside the town hall, near where the original Sand Rock schoolhouse once stood. Overall, the place gives off kind of a "same, but different" feel. It is the same sense visitors to the new field house get when they glance at the man sitting behind the desk in the head coach's office.

Almost twenty-five years after his Wildcats won the state championship, Russell Jacoway still paces the sideline. He has a few more gray hairs and a couple of grandchildren now, but he rides his bike in the off-season and keeps himself in shape. Just to prove that 1985 was no fluke, he led Sand Rock to another state title game. "The team from the year before was probably a better team, overall," said Jacoway, whose Wildcats had to settle for second place in 1997. "We just didn't get the breaks in 1996 that we did in '97." Jacoway's assistant coaches (he has seven of them now) will tell you he has mellowed slightly over the years…but only slightly. Like any coach worth his salt, Jacoway still wants to win every game.

Kenny Beck has been around Russell Jacoway since he began keeping team statistics in 1995. After leaving the military, Beck became an assistant coach for Jacoway in 2005. Based on his own experience, Beck said that he offered Jacoway a little advice about sensing when the time is right to step away. "I told him he had better make sure he no longer wants to be the man in charge," Beck said. "I don't see him being that way yet. He still enjoys coaching and still does such a good job of delegating authority, right down to doing the laundry and cutting off the stadium lights. He still has a lot of fire for what he does. He knows the people around him are going to do their jobs and it makes more time for him to coach football, which is what he really loves."

In some ways, October 30, 2009, was a special night for Russell Jacoway. But in other ways, it was a complete letdown. Despite entering the final game of the season with a winning record, the Wildcats lost one too many games, so coaches and players already knew that regardless of the outcome against Spring Garden, they would be excluded from the state playoffs. On the other hand, Coach Jacoway was sitting on 199 career wins and relished his last chance (for several months, anyway) to reach the magic number that had driven him since junior high, when he was sketching plays instead of studying his lessons. He has kept the dream alive at Sand Rock season after season as offers for jobs at bigger schools have come and gone. Content with his life on Lookout Mountain,

Jacoway has looked to his wife, Yvonne, for reassurance and then waved off every opportunity.

Yvonne claims that one of the hardest things she ever did was learn how to live on Lookout Mountain after moving there in 1983. "It is different, and you don't realize it until you live here," she said. "Sometimes people think I'm crazy when I say this, but these are tougher people. They live harder, but they're also very generous people." That generosity engulfed the Jacoways not long after they first arrived in Sand Rock. Russell and Yvonne were making it "by the skin of our teeth" in the early going, living mainly on the small amount of money she had pulled out of her Georgia teacher's retirement fund.

Not long after getting set up in their first house, "the water heater went out and we had no money and no way to come up with it," Yvonne said. "The community heard that we needed a water heater, so they took up a collection and bought us one. They took care of us, and I think that knowing they were willing to do that for us helped to reassure us we were in the right place." Many times since, that same feeling has served to reassure the Jacoways of the wisdom of their decision, made repeatedly through the years, to continue their lives atop Lookout Mountain. Yvonne said that her husband always trusted her gut feeling whenever it came to career advancement. Several offers came over the years, but none ever seemed to be the right place at the right time. "This is where we're supposed to be," she said. "It's worked out pretty well." Always the coach's wife, she smiled before adding: "So far."

So far, at 4:30 pm, on the afternoon of Coach Jacoway's latest opportunity to win his 200th career game, everything is looking pretty good. After school lets out for the day, Jacoway and his assistants supervise a final walkthrough. The mood is light, and the players seem prepared to take a whack at the latest curveball their head coach has thrown their way. Setting aside the spread option offense his Wildcats have run with success for most of the season, Jacoway has dug deep into his playbook and pulled out an offensive formation used only sparingly in recent years. Instead of players sprinting back and forth across multiple-receiver formations or a mass of misdirection handoffs in the backfield, Jacoway wants to see if his boys can line up against the Panthers and simply grind them into the ground. "The huddling and the power-I formation is stuff we did for years here," Jacoway says after the game. "We went back to that and it helped us a lot, I think, from the aspect of being more physical."

After the players spend about thirty minutes on the field in shorts and T-shirts going over offensive and defensive formations, the walkthrough ends and Jacoway allows his eccentric side to show. Like many athletes and coaches, Jacoway has accumulated several superstitious routines through the years. For a long time, he personally handled every ball and roll of tape packed for road trips and drove around the neighborhood with the window rolled down on Thursday nights before home games. "I felt like I had to touch every single thing that we were taking with us," he said about the packing ritual. "And the kids always thought I was driving around at night to see if I could find someone who was out doing something they weren't supposed to be doing, but I was really just listening to the radio and collecting my thoughts for the game."

Over the years, Jacoway has turned over many pre-game duties to assistant coaches and let go of some of his superstitions, but at least one remains. As has been the rule since 1983, only the head coach is allowed to climb into the top level of the press box on home game Friday nights and hit the power switch that brings the sound system to life. (The old cassette deck has long since given way to a new iPod docking station, but for two hours before kickoff and whenever the Wildcats win, "We Will Rock You" still reverberates across Lookout Mountain just as if it has been delivered, circa-1985, by Doc Brown's flying DeLorean.)

Thirty minutes before kickoff, as players perform pre-game rituals of their own along the sideline, James Rowe ambles through the gate and heads toward Jacoway. The two still share a special bond, and Rowe knows that he is welcome on the field any time. (After all, that patch of grass used to be his office, too.) The two men share a few words before punctuating the air with a friendly laugh. Rowe wishes Jacoway good luck as he heads back to the sideline fence, his regular spot for watching the Wildcats since retiring from teaching and coaching in 1996. During their talk, Jacoway shares his plan to begin the game with the same offensive formation the Wildcats once employed so successfully, and Rowe relishes the nostalgic aspect of the strategy he is about to see unfold. "Some of these kids have never even taken a snap under center," he says. "The spread is nothing more than a fast-break offense, like in basketball." If anyone in the crowd can appreciate Jacoway's surprise game plan, it is Rowe.

When the game begins, the Wildcats break the huddle, and the Spring Garden defenders are caught completely off-guard. This simple, smash-mouth offense is nothing like the Sand Rock team they have seen on film all week. Eight plays after taking the opening kickoff, sophomore Chad Thompson scores on a six-yard run, and Matthew Cole adds the point-after. The ground pounding continues in the second quarter, when senior fullback Wesley Pruitt rambles thirty-four yards, increasing the Wildcats' lead to 14–0. A few minutes later, just as Spring Garden begins to get a handle on Sand Rock's power-I, Jacoway instructs coordinator Steven Chesnut to revert back to the Wildcats' typical, wide-open attack. Quarterback Drew Norris—whose father, Eddie, played on Jim Lowery's state playoff team in 1981—fires a short pass to senior Phillip Washburn, who turns the play into a sixty-yard touchdown. "When we changed

Running back Wesley Pruitt exemplified Sand Rock's temporary return to smash-mouth football with his touchdown in the first half of Russell Jacoway's two hundredth career win. The final score was 30–0. *Photo by Stanley Carlton.*

pace and went back to the no-huddle, I think that hurt them a little bit," Jacoway says later. Midway through the third, Cole boots a short field goal. Then, on the Wildcats' next possession, Norris completes a long touchdown pass to Justin Kyser to close out the scoring and secure Jacoway's historic win.

Several former Wildcats are in the bleachers, and more than one is on the sideline. Jim Tom Stimpson, true to his promise to give back to the school that loved him, warts and all, volunteers as the team statistician on Friday nights. The former running back follows the football up and down the sideline, electronically recording yards gained and tackles for loss. All-State quarterback Lance Mackey, who has two young sons working their way into Jacoway's starting lineup, is a member of the athletic boosters club and spends the night marking down and distance as one of the three-man chain crew. On his way back from the concession stand during halftime, Mackey stops by the flagpole, where former players always gather, and says hello to several old teammates. As he reenters the

Russell Jacoway dodges a bucket of ice water as his players and assistants look on. Fourteen seconds later, the fifty-two-year-old coach reached a career milestone that he had been dreaming of since eighth grade. *Photo by Stanley Carlton.*

field, Mackey bumps into former assistant Roland Hendon. Now retired from teaching and working for a photography studio, Hendon, like Rowe, still watches the game with a coach's eye and prefers a ground-level spot along the fence. For two old football coaches, the bleachers are simply too far away from the action.

It seems appropriate that so many who were a part of Russell Jacoway's first win at Sand Rock are present the night he takes his place in Alabama high school football history. Public address announcer Terry Teat, still a reasonable resemblance of the young man who took part in the television broadcast of Jacoway's twenty-third win, is the first to officially announce the achievement of his 200th. After dodging a cooler of ice water, Jacoway heads to midfield to receive the first of many congratulatory handshakes. Jason Howard, already the most successful head coach in Spring Garden football history, almost seems content to be the honored victim. "My opinion, he's the best coach in northeast Alabama, if not the whole state," Howard says as he stands near midfield after a friendly post-game chat with Jacoway. "I give him a hard time about being the old man around here, but that old man still kicks all our butts every chance he gets."

Steve Smith, the head coach of the 2009 Class 3A state champion Piedmont Bulldogs, was a rookie head coach at Cedar Bluff in 1995. Smith remembered how, despite the intense rivalry between the Tigers and Wildcats, Jacoway was quick to help him get comfortable in his new position. "When I started out, [Sand Rock] was right in the middle of a run in the late 1990s where they were in the quarterfinals and semifinals every year, but Coach Jacoway took a lot of time out of his schedule to offer me assistance and advice on being a head coach."

Smith said he has always had respect for what Jacoway has been able to accomplish at Sand Rock. "I don't mean this as a slight in any way, but I have watched him do more with less, for years, than any other coach I know of. Over the years he has won a lot of games that probably, on paper, he should have lost. I always tell people that any halfway decent coach can win with talent. He's won with scrappy, hard-nosed football players. They have been loyal to him and he's been loyal back to them."

Smith said that anyone who is looking to break into the hard-knock world of coaching would do well to take a long, hard look at what Jacoway has accomplished over the years. "He's been the model of what a good

On the night Russell Jacoway won his two hundredth game, Lance Mackey (right) was the first former player to congratulate the man who had shown so much confidence in him a generation before. *Photo by Vickie Reeves.*

football coach is all about. He's probably had plenty of chances to go to other places for more money over the years, but he's planted himself in that community and he's done an outstanding job," Smith said. "I respect him as much as a person as I do as a football coach."

According to Jacoway, Steve Smith and Jason Howard—along with plenty of other coaches across northeast Alabama—will continue having to deal with the "old man" from Lookout Mountain for the foreseeable future. "I'm still fired up about coaching," Jacoway says as he stands in the middle of a room filled with family, friends and former players after the game. "I may not move as fast as I used to, but I'm not planning on going anywhere anytime soon." Among the men in attendance is Yvonne Jacoway's father, Hershel Burt, perhaps the biggest Wildcat fan of them all. Home or away, bright September sunshine or mind-numbing November cold, he has been in the bleachers for every single Sand Rock football game since the day his son-in-law got the job.

Russell Jacoway with (from left) his father-in-law, wife Yvonne, daughters Christina Jacoway and Amy Cox and grandsons Gaitlin Cox and Gunner Cox, on October 30, 2009. Yvonne's father, Hershel Burt, has attended every single game his son-in-law has ever coached. *Photo by Vickie Reeves.*

When Dan Andrews, a junior on the 1985 state championship team, pokes his head through a post-game crowd of reporters and well-wishers to offer his congratulations, there is feeling in his voice. As soon as Jacoway looks around and sees his former player, his reaction is immediate and involuntary.

He is not among those gathered, but if he were, Artie Mackey would surely recognize what is happening. He witnessed a similar expression of emotion in Russell Jacoway's eyes once before, a long time ago, in a jampacked locker room on a chilly, December night in Repton, Alabama.

INDEX

D

F

G

H

J

K

L

M

N

P

R

S

T

V

W

Y

ABOUT THE AUTHOR

Scott Wright graduated from the University of Alabama in 1993. He is the managing editor of the *Post*, a weekly newspaper in Centre, Alabama. He is the author of *A History of Weiss Lake*, also from The History Press. To contact Scott, please send an email to swright@postpaper.com.

www.ingramcontent.com/pod-product-compliance
Lightning Source LLC
LaVergne TN
LVHW010949100826
845153LV00002B/178

* 9 7 8 1 5 4 0 2 3 4 5 7 5 *